Social Structures and the Making of Museveni's Civil-Authoritarian Regime in Uganda

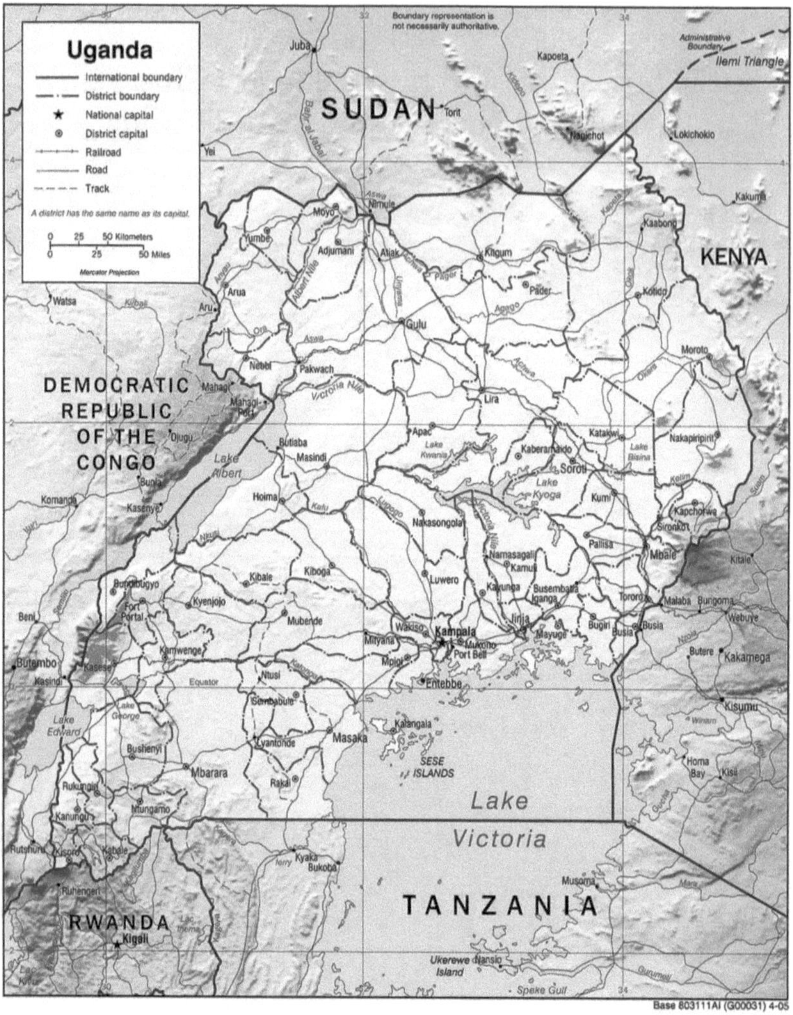

Map of Uganda (*Source* Guide of the world)

Gerald Bareebe

Social Structures and the Making of Museveni's Civil-Authoritarian Regime in Uganda

palgrave
macmillan

Gerald Bareebe
Department of Politics
York University
Toronto, ON, Canada

ISBN 978-3-032-14014-2 ISBN 978-3-032-14015-9 (eBook)
https://doi.org/10.1007/978-3-032-14015-9

Cover credit: The Daily Monitor

This Palgrave Macmillan imprint is published by the registered company Springer Nature Switzerland AG
The registered company address is: Gewerbestrasse 11, 6330 Cham, Switzerland

To my late father, Vincent Musinguzi, whose love and guidance continue to shape all that I do.

Foreword

As Uganda's ruling National Resistance Movement (NRM) prepares to celebrate its 40th anniversary in power, observers want to know how longtime President Yoweri Museveni has maintained relative stability, regime resilience, and durability amidst widespread post-colonial fragility across the rest of the African continent. In this book, Gerald Bareebe takes a bite at the complex strands of political, social, and economic explanatory variables linked to the mechanics of rule in Uganda's political dispensation. In so doing, he demystifies Museveni's long political "shelf life" by credibly claiming that his ingenuity is rooted in the construction of a "distinctive civil-authoritarian" regime—"authoritarian" in that it is hegemonic, and "civil" in that it is underpinned by manipulation of (or bargains with) "residual social structures." The latter comprises institutions of social organization that have endured over time and continue to frame elite behavior and political culture. If "civil authoritarianism" were a tree, the trunk would consist of several rings: patronage, militarization, containment, state building, and political settlements driven by political self-preservation.

The intellectual depth of the book is best appreciated by joining Bareebe in his investigation into a) the NRM's historical build up toward civil authoritarianism, b) its penchant for coercion, co-optation, and neutralization of armed rivals, c) Museveni's capacity to defang social opposition groups while simultaneously curtailing their capacity to engage processes of statehood negotiations meaningfully, d) the regime's adeptness at applying correction and accommodation as apparatus for anchoring its political settlements, and e) how repression is outsourced to shadowy vigilante and third party actors.

The author concludes with a thoughtful discussion of postwar authoritarianism and how the Uganda case informs the broader body of intellectual inquiry into the paucity of liberal democratic institutions and governance in Africa. The conclusion is notable for reminding the reader of an earlier conversation initiated by the preeminent scholar Rebecca Tapscott (2021), whose concept of modern authoritarianism seems to have inspired Bareebe to delve deeper into the NRM regime's subterranean underbelly. Thus, both scholars invite us to deconstruct the evolving (and sometimes paradoxical) mutations of power in Uganda and across Africa.

Overall, this book makes a significant contribution to the already extensive body of scholarly research on the evolution of illiberal democracy in Africa. It fills critical gaps left by a corpus of scholarship, including, inter alia, the following: Rubongoya 2007, 2025; Weigratz 2016; Khisa et al. 2016; Mamdani (1996), et al. The latter have researched the continuation and contradictions of authoritarianism in Uganda. However, the broader historical context of Bareebe's work is found in earlier works by intellectual luminaries such as Young (1994, 2012), Kasfir (1976), Kasozi (1994), Karugire (1980), et al.

Bareebe's presuppositions and arguments are authentic and persuasive, especially given the depth of his scholarship (2016, 2019, 2020, 2021, 2023, 2024) on Uganda's political trajectory. A native of Uganda, Bareebe amplifies a particularly audible and compelling contribution to a genre of scholarship dating back to 1986, when Museveni seized power after a 5-year guerrilla struggle. Also, he raises profound questions for further inquiry and debate. Finally, considering the ongoing global shift toward right-wing autocracy, Bareebe may be talking to the global south while implicitly asking the north to "turn the volume up."

Salem, VA, USA
December 27, 2025

Joshua B. Rubongoya, PhD
Rubongoy@roanoke.edu

Acknowledgments This book would not have been possible without the support of many people whom I deeply value. My wife, Joan Besigye, encouraged and supported me from the moment the idea of this book first took shape. I am grateful for her patience, kindness, and moral support, which were instrumental to the completion of this work. To our young children, Jadrien and Hailey—thank you for the joy and inspiration you bring to our lives.

A major inspiration for this book was my doctoral advisor and mentor, Prof. Antoinette Handley at the University of Toronto. Her guidance, insightful suggestions, and unwavering support shaped both my research and my development as a scholar and teacher. I am also thankful to Prof. Nakanyike B. Musisi for engaging in countless discussions on Uganda's political developments, and to Dr. Lwanga Musisi, whose extensive experience within both the NRM and the National Unity Platform offered invaluable perspectives. You are both extraordinary colleagues and lifelong friends.

I am grateful to colleagues at the University of Toronto and York University, particularly Prof. Dickson Eyoh and Prof. Karen Murray, for their support throughout my academic career. I also thank Prof. Shingirai L. Taodzera at the University of California, Davis, for generously sharing insights during our many discussions and collaborative projects, including the joint research conference at Makerere University in Kampala, Uganda. I am especially thankful to Prof. Rita Abrahamsen at Ottawa university, with whom I have collaborated on research and publications. Working with you has been an invaluable learning experience. Her mentorship and collaboration have profoundly shaped my development as a scholar and writer.

Last but certainly not least, I wish to express my sincere gratitude to Professor Moses Khisa of North Carolina State University. Our extensive discussions on the nature of the ruling NRM regime offered critical insights that greatly shaped the development of this work. I am also deeply grateful to all my respondents in Uganda—politicians, journalists, civil society actors, as well as leaders from various kingdoms and religious institutions—who generously shared their time and perspectives during my fieldwork.

Competing Interests The author has no competing interests to declare that are relevant to the content of this manuscript.

Contents

About the Author

Gerald Bareebe is an Associate Professor in the Department of Politics at York University, Canada. His research and teaching focus on politics and government, international relations, civil wars, and the comparative politics of the Global South. He holds a PhD in Political Science from the University of Toronto, as well as master's degrees in international relations from Makerere University and in Governance and Development from the University of Antwerp. His work has appeared in leading international journals, including *African Affairs*, *Civil Wars*, *Commonwealth & Comparative Politics*, and the *Journal of Democracy*, as well as in several edited volumes on African and comparative politics.

Acronyms and Abbreviations

AC	Army Council
ADF	Allied Democratic Forces
ARLPI	Acholi Religious Leaders Peace Initiative
AU	African Union
CA	Constituent Assembly
CAO	Chief Administrative Officer
CAR	Central African Republic
CBR	Central Bank Rate
CID	Criminal Investigation Department
CMI	Chieftaincy of Military Intelligence
CPP	Crime Preventers Program
DFID	Department for International Development
DIC	District Intelligence Committees
DP	Democratic Party
DPP	Director of Public Prosecutions
DRC	Democratic Republic of the Congo
DSC	District Security Committee
EC	Electoral Commission
EFD	Electronic Fiscal Device
EFRIS	Electronic Fiscal Receipting and Invoicing Solution
EPRDF	Ethiopian People's Revolutionary Democratic Front
ESO	External Security Organization
FDC	Forum for Democratic Change
FEDEMU	Federal Democratic Movement of Uganda
FRELIMO	Front for the Liberation of Mozambique
FRONASA	Front for National Salvation

GDP	Gross Domestic Product
GKMA	Greater Kampala Metropolitan Area
HC	High Command
HRW	Human Rights Watch
HSMF	Holy Spirit Mobile Force
IMF	International Monetary Fund
ISO	Internal Security Organization
JATF	Joint Anti-Terrorism Task Force
JIC	Joint Intelligence Committee
KACITA	Kampala City Traders Association
KAP	Kalangala Action Plan
KCPS	Kampala Central Police Station
LC	Local Council
LDU	Local Defence Unit
MP	Member of Parliament
NALU	National Army for the Liberation of Uganda
NEC	National Executive Committee
NRA	National Resistance Army
NRC	National Resistance Council
NRM	National Resistance Movement
NRM/A	National Resistance Movement/Army
NRM-O	National Resistance Movement–Organization
NSC	National Security Council
NUP	National Unity Platform
PAFO	Parliamentary Advocacy Forum
PGB	Presidential Guard Brigade
POMA	Public Order Management Act
PPU	Presidential Protection Unit
PRA	Popular Resistance Army
PVoC	Pre-export Verification of Conformity
RA	Reform Agenda
RDC	Resident District Commissioner
RPA	Rwandan Patriotic Army
RPF	Rwandan Patriotic Front
SFC	Special Forces Command
SPLA	Sudan People's Liberation Army
SSC	Sub-County Security Committee
UFM	Uganda Freedom Movement
UG	Uganda
UGSHS	Uganda Shillings
UHRC	Uganda Human Rights Commission
UN	United Nations
UNA	Uganda National Army

UNLA	Uganda National Liberation Army
UNLF	Uganda National Liberation Front
UPC	Uganda People's Congress
UPDA	Uganda People's Democratic Army
UPDF	Uganda People's Defence Forces
UPDM/A	Uganda People's Democratic Movement/Army
UPM	Uganda Patriotic Movement
URA	Uganda Revenue Authority
VAT	Value Added Tax
WNBF	West Nile Bank Front
ZANU	Zimbabwe African National Union

PART I

Residual Social Structures and Consolidation of NRM Rule

CHAPTER 1

The Evolution and Trajectories of the NRM Regime in Post-conflict Uganda

Uganda's post-independence trajectory, like that of many African nations, has been marked by enduring structural and political crises stemming from colonial legacies and state fragility. Following its independence in 1962, Uganda quickly descended into political instability, marked by the erosion of constitutional order and the consolidation of autocratic rule.[1] The military coup of 1971, which brought Idi Amin to power, ushered in one of the most violent and repressive regimes in postcolonial African history. Amin's regime (1971–1979) was characterized by the collapse of state institutions and widespread human rights violations, including extra-judicial killings, ethnic persecution, mass disappearances, torture, and the arbitrary detention of political opponents.[2]

Under Amin's rule, security agencies operated with impunity, systematically targeting journalists, academics, religious leaders, and members of marginalized ethnic groups perceived as hostile to the regime—most notably the Acholi, Langi and other tribes. An estimated 300,000 Ugandans were killed under his regime, while key sectors of the economy, especially those owned by the expelled Asian business community were decimated, plunging the country into economic collapse.[3]

The ouster of Idi Amin in 1979 by a coalition of Tanzanian forces and Ugandan exiles did not produce a peaceful or stable transition.[4] Instead, it created a power vacuum that unleashed further violence and

G. Bareebe, *Social Structures and the Making of Museveni's Civil-Authoritarian Regime in Uganda*,
https://doi.org/10.1007/978-3-032-14015-9_1

deepened political fragmentation. Between 1979 and 1986, Uganda experienced recurrent regime changes, chronic insecurity, contested electoral processes, and the proliferation of armed groups.[5] The fraudulent 1980 elections returned Milton Obote to power, triggering renewed civil conflict.[6] The most significant armed opposition to Obote's second regime came from Yoweri Museveni's National Resistance Army (NRA), which launched a protracted guerrilla insurgency in response to what it viewed as gross electoral malpractice in the 1980 general elections.

Obote's second presidency (1980–1985) reproduced many of the governance failures that had defined his first rule (1966–1971).[7] It was marked by rampant corruption, patronage-driven politics, ethnic exclusion, and militarized repression, factors that further exacerbated Uganda's political crisis. Obote's government carried out brutal counterinsurgency operations—particularly in the Luwero Triangle—where it employed scorched-earth tactics against communities suspected of supporting the NRA.[8] These campaigns resulted in the mass killing of civilians and further eroded the state's legitimacy in the eyes of the population.

Uganda's experience during this period reflected broader patterns observed across postcolonial Africa, including the failure to establish inclusive and effective governance structures, the personalization of political power, and the strategic manipulation of ethnic divisions to consolidate authority.[9] These dynamics not only fostered persistent violence but also eroded social cohesion and undermined the state's administrative and coercive capacities. Across the continent, similar trajectories unfolded. For example, in Liberia, the collapse of state authority and ethnic rivalries fueled the outbreak of a brutal civil war in 1989.[10] In Sierra Leone, political corruption and marginalization triggered an insurgency in 1991 that led to a decade-long conflict marked by widespread atrocities.[11] Ethiopia experienced violent regime change and a devastating civil war which culminated in the fall of the Derg regime in 1991[12] after a successful military campaign by the Ethiopian People's Revolutionary Democratic Front (EPRDF).[13] In Sudan, the continuation of North–South conflict after the Addis Ababa Agreement collapsed in 1983 reignited a protracted civil war.[14] Meanwhile, in Rwanda and Burundi, cycles of ethnic violence culminated in the 1994 genocide and recurring massacres.[15] These cases underscore the inherent fragility of postcolonial African states, that was fundamentally characterized by exclusionary identity politics and the entrenchment of militarized governance. Such conditions precipitated widespread insecurity, the disintegration of institutional frameworks, and persistent economic stagnation across the continent during the 1980s and 1990s.[16]

As in many other African countries, Uganda's political disintegration created conditions conducive to protracted insurgency and entrenched state repression, ultimately enabling the NRA's capture of power in 1986 through a successful guerrilla warfare.[17] However, the NRA's rise to power did not swiftly usher in political stability. The nascent regime grappled with persistent insurgencies, localized uprisings, and widespread civil unrest, all of which significantly impeded its efforts to consolidate state authority and achieve national pacification. State failure aggravated internal divisions and heightened contestation over the state's legitimate monopoly on violence. Fundamentally, the emergent regime confronted two critical challenges: first, how to establish an effective monopoly over coercive force; and second, how to cultivate a durable foundation of political legitimacy by assembling a capable and broadly credible coalition committed to effective governance and national unity. As a result, the Ugandan state after 1986 remained structurally fragile, frequently failing to deliver essential public services and, in critical instances, proving either institutionally incapable or politically unwilling to curb the excesses of its military and security forces.

Recognizing the entrenched roots of prior political instability, the NRA sought to steer Uganda in a new direction. President Yoweri Museveni pursued a strategy of co-optation, selective accommodation, and strategic concessions aimed at aligning the regime with entrenched, pre-existing social and political structures. This approach sought to fragment and manage the political space in ways that diffused dissent without threatening regime dominance. Consequently, a civil-authoritarian order gradually emerged—one in which the military, though still a cornerstone of state power, became increasingly subordinated to the broader political objectives of the ruling elite. This configuration enabled the regime to consolidate authority, marginalize opposition, and institutionalize authoritarian rule within a nominally civilian framework.

This book advances a set of interrelated arguments about the nature of post-conflict governance in Uganda. It begins by challenging the assumption that the NRA military victory in 1986 constituted a complete institutional rupture and enabled the unencumbered construction of a new political order. Rather, I argue that the NRA—later institutionalized as the National Resistance Movement (NRM) party—inherited what I term a "residual" social structure; a landscape shaped by the persistence and continued influence of longstanding social formations. Among these were influential religious institutions such as the Protestant and Catholic churches, landed elites, traditional monarchies, and historic political parties that had weathered the turbulence of Uganda's civil wars.

Faced with the enduring authority of entrenched social groups, the NRM was compelled to pursue a strategy grounded in co-optation, collaboration, and concession. Rather than dismantling these forces, the regime integrated them into a recalibrated political configuration best understood as a civil-authoritarian order—an adaptive and pragmatic mode of governance that absorbs diverse societal interests within an authoritarian framework. Over time, President Museveni has increasingly recognized that overt repression of these influential actors carries significant political risks and threatens regime stability. Consequently, while coercion remains a key instrument of rule, the regime has progressively leaned on non-coercive mechanisms—including elite accommodation, coalition-building, and strategic concessions—to mitigate dissent and consolidate power.

This is not to suggest, however, that the NRM eschews coercion altogether. On the contrary, violence remains a central instrument of rule, albeit one that is often outsourced or obfuscated. Rather than relying solely on the formal coercive apparatus of the state, the regime frequently delegates violence to third-party actors—including vigilante groups, semi-official militias, and paramilitary networks—as a way of insulating itself from direct accountability. Organizations such as the Kiboko Squad, Kalangala Action Plan, and the Crime Preventers have functioned as key enforcers of regime stability, operating within the grey zones of state-sanctioned violence while allowing the central government to deny responsibility for their excesses. These hybrid security arrangements have become integral to the resilience and durability of Museveni's regime.

Therefore, the reconstruction of Uganda's post-war political order followed a distinct trajectory compared to other post-conflict regimes in the region. A particularly instructive contrast can be drawn with Rwanda, where the Rwandan Patriotic Army (RPA) emerged from the 1994 genocide into a fundamentally altered social landscape. Unlike the NRA, which confronted a resilient "residual" social structure composed of entrenched elites, religious institutions, monarchies, and historical political parties, the RPA entered a near-total political vacuum. In Rwanda, most members of the pre-genocide elite—who had previously controlled the state—were either killed, captured, or forced into exile during and after the genocide. This rupture marked a critical watershed, effectively eliminating rival power centers and enabling the RPA to consolidate control over the new state and society with minimal resistance from pre-existing social forces.

This contrast underscores the foundational influence of pre-existing social structures in shaping both the character and strategic choices of authoritarian statecraft. In Uganda, the persistence of entrenched social groups has imposed significant constraints on the post-war NRA/NRM regime. Rather than ruling through sheer coercion, the regime has been compelled to adopt a hybrid governance model—one that blends overt and covert forms of coercion with non-coercive strategies such as accommodation, alliance-building, and selective patronage. These civil-authoritarian arrangements reflect a political order shaped not solely by military power but also by the need to manage and negotiate with historically rooted social forces. In contrast, military-dominated regimes such as Rwanda's operate in fundamentally different conditions. The near-total collapse of pre-existing social structures in the aftermath of the genocide allowed the RPA to assert uncontested dominance, enabling the regime to consolidate power with minimal resistance. Inheriting a sociopolitical vacuum, such regimes face fewer constraints from residual social actors and are consequently more inclined to rely on direct coercion as their main instrument of governance.

Methodologically, this book is grounded in an in-depth, single-country case study of Uganda, which enables both rich empirical description and robust analytical insight. This approach is particularly well-suited to uncovering the complex interplay between formal institutions and informal power dynamics—an interaction that lies at the heart of the analysis. The research draws on data collected over four rounds of fieldwork conducted in Uganda between 2017 and 2024. During this period, I conducted a series of formal and informal key informant interviews with actors across political, social, and bureaucratic domains. These interviews provided valuable first-hand perspectives on regime dynamics, elite strategies, and the evolving character of state–society relations.

To enhance the credibility and breadth of data collection, interviews were triangulated with a wide array of secondary sources, including media reports, government documents, press releases, and policy publications from civil society organizations and international NGOs. This allowed systematic assessment of long-term political trends and regime trajectories, both within Uganda and in the broader regional context. In addressing particularly sensitive topics—such as national security, informal coercive practices, and the role of powerful elites—I relied on informal interviews arranged through personal networks, including confidential conversations with well-placed individuals in government and elite social circles. These interviews, though some anonymized for ethical and safety reasons, were essential for shedding light on otherwise opaque aspects of regime behavior. Taken together, the data sources underpin a grounded explanation of how Uganda's residual social structure shaped the formation and evolution of the NM's authoritarian character. This empirical foundation enables a broader reflection on the implications of social embeddedness for state consolidation, governance, and development in post-conflict settings. The findings demonstrate why Uganda's path to regime consolidation diverged significantly from other cases in the region.

Uganda offers a compelling case for examining state reconstruction and regime consolidation in the aftermath of protracted civil war, as it encapsulates the multifaceted challenges confronting post-colonial African states. Its historical trajectory reveals how state failure emerges from a confluence of political, economic, and colonial legacies. Politically, the post-independence period was characterized by weak institutions and intense power struggles, notably under the regimes of Milton Obote and Idi Amin, which deepened the crisis of governance. Economically, colonial-era distortions created structural vulnerabilities that persisted into the post-independence era. These were exacerbated by the politicization of ethnic identities during colonial rule, fueling cycles of instability. External interventions further undermined state-building efforts across Africa. In Uganda, as elsewhere on the continent, Western powers often imposed destabilizing economic reforms—such as structural adjustment programs—and pursued Cold War-era geopolitical interests that prioritized regime survival over institutional development. In countries like Rwanda, Sudan, Ethiopia, and Angola, foreign support to specific regimes or rebel groups frequently disrupted fragile governance structures. By channeling aid, military backing, or ideological agendas to select actors, external powers amplified internal divisions, fostered corruption, and deepened economic dependency. These dynamics underscore the enduring dilemmas of post-colonial state formation and development, which the next section interrogates in greater depth.

Colonial Legacies and the Crisis of African Statehood

Since the end of colonialism, the African state has remained mired in civil conflicts driven by repression, ethnicity, secessionism, irredentism, and nationalism.[18] Political elites have frequently exploited ethnopolitical cleavages to destabilize state institutions, marginalize minority groups, and incite ethnic hatred. These challenges are rooted in colonial partition policies that arbitrarily split ethnic communities and amalgamated distinct groups into newly created states that neither reflected their cultural heritage nor political aspirations. Many ethnic groups were forced into political entities governed by alien values, institutions, and norms.[19] As a result, postcolonial states emerged structurally fragile, overcentralized, internally divided, and lacking legitimacy in the eyes of their citizens. Coercion, rather than popular consent, became the principal basis of state authority.

Understanding the structural weaknesses of postcolonial African states necessitates a critical engagement with the multifaceted legacies of colonialism—political, economic, social, and aesthetic. Competing theoretical frameworks offer divergent interpretations of the postcolonial state's condition and trajectory. Liberal perspectives, for example, often view the African state as socioeconomically underdeveloped and in need of transformation toward liberal modernity.[20] In pursuit of this model, Western donor states and development agencies exerted pressure on post-independence African regimes to engage in institution-building. Efforts to establish legislatures, judicial systems, political parties, and security apparatuses were framed as pathways to decolonizing the state and embedding indigenous legitimacy. Such initiatives reflected a normative belief in the universal applicability of liberal institutionalism, even as they frequently overlooked local complexities and the enduring imprint of colonial rule.

The arbitrary colonial demarcation of borders fractured communities and undermined the possibility of building cohesive national identities.[21] Despite the continent's rich socio-linguistic diversity, most African states lacked a unified sense of nationhood. Communities continued to identify primarily through kinship, shared ancestry, language, and customs, social bonds that could have served as a foundation for nation-building. Instead, tensions between competing identities—citizenship, ethnicity, nationalism, tradition, and modernity—intensified in the post-independence era, often culminating in civil wars. These crises were, in many ways, a continuation of the colonial legacy, particularly the disruptions of late colonialism.[22] As a result, scholars describe the political trajectory of postcolonial African states as oscillating between hope and disillusionment. Crawford Young, for example, underscores the cycle of optimism and despair that characterizes Africa's post-independence political evolution.[23] The euphoria that accompanied independence in the 1960s was swiftly eroded by the rise of authoritarian single-party regimes and military dictatorships across the continent.[24] Most newly independent states proved ill-equipped to manage internal challenges of state formation or to respond effectively to growing political and economic crises.

Postcolonial state-builders faced the formidable challenge of cultivating a cohesive national identity amidst societies fractured by colonial legacies and deeply rooted social, political, and economic divisions. These enduring cleavages complicated efforts to construct inclusive political communities and coherent national narratives, rendering the task of post-independence state-building both precarious and contested. Many scholars and international actors advocated for the adoption of neoliberal models of governance, assuming that replicating Western institutional frameworks would strengthen the African state. Consequently, most African countries adopted liberal democratic institutions and policies. However, the fusion of Western governance models with local realities often generated internal tensions.[25] For instance, while democracy was externally promoted, it frequently became a source of political instability and inter-communal conflict. Many African states lacked the capacity to govern effectively as they could neither assert control over their full territory, provide essential public goods, nor assert a monopoly on the legitimate exercise of violence. Consequently, prolonged civil conflicts erupted across the continent, rooted in political polarization and state weakness.[26]

By the late 1970s and early 1980s, many African states that had gained independence amidst great optimism and celebration had descended into acute political crises and socioeconomic stagnation.[27] Several interrelated factors contributed to the continental crisis of this period. These included the divisive legacy of colonial rule, which entrenched tribal and ethnic cleavages; Cold War rivalries that turned Africa into a theater of ideological competition and proxy wars; the absence of coherent, homegrown nation-building visions; and the imposition of externally inspired economic models—such as liberal structural adjustment policies—that often clashed with local political and social realities. Postcolonial regimes, rather than transforming inherited colonial structures, frequently reinforced authoritarian and exclusionary governance through clientelism, tribalism, nepotism, and patrimonialism. Lacking accountability and legitimacy, many governments adopted policies that further alienated their populations. The result was the proliferation of insurgent movements seeking to overthrow incumbent regimes, which further accelerated state fragility and undermining institutional cohesion.

Ethnic politics and ethnonationalist mobilization played a central role in the deterioration of African states during the 1970s and 1980s periods. The colonial project had already laid the groundwork for inter-ethnic tensions by privileging and marginalizing certain groups over others and manipulating ethnic hierarchies. Post-independence leaders, rather than diffusing these tensions, often resorted to exclusionary strategies to consolidate power, marginalizing ethnic groups they perceived as threats. These policies triggered widespread resentment and, in many cases, armed rebellion. The situation was exacerbated by competition over scarce resources, divergent cultural values, contested state legitimacy, and the rise of ideological extremism. As state capacity eroded, many governments became increasingly dependent on external support for survival, often failing to provide basic security or protect their citizens from escalating violence.[28]

The Cold War significantly intensified the African state crisis of the 1980s and 1990s.[29] The United States and the Soviet Union, eager to secure influence in postcolonial Africa, provided military, financial, and political support to rival factions and client regimes. These interventions transformed localized conflicts into prolonged proxy wars, destabilizing fragile postcolonial states. Major conflicts such as the Congo Crisis (1960–1965),[30] the Ethio-Somali War (1977–1978), the Angolan Civil War (1975–2002), and the Mozambican Civil War (1977–1992) were all fueled by Cold War rivalries.[31] The influx of arms and resources from foreign powers empowered rebel leaders, warlords and militias to wage brutal campaigns over control of natural resources in countries such as Congo, Sierra Leone, and Liberia.[32]

Consequently, the number of African states embroiled in violent conflict peaked during this period. State authority became deeply contested, and the monopoly on the legitimate use of violence—central to the Weberian conception of statehood—was fractured. In many cases, government forces engaged in protracted battles with insurgent groups, while in others, the state itself fragmented under the pressure of civil war. Even in countries that avoided large-scale conflict, state institutions remained fragile and vulnerable to both internal and external shocks. The outcomes varied across the continent. In some states, insurgents succeeded in seizing power, achieving secession, or staging successful coups d'état. In others, incumbent regimes prevailed militarily but at great cost to stability and legitimacy. Several states remained trapped in chronic crisis conditions, while others including Uganda began to recover, transitioning into periods of relative peace and political stabilization.

Foundations of Post-1986 NRM Civil-Authoritarianism

Since the end of the NRA civil war, Uganda has experienced a period of relative political stability and socioeconomic recovery. This enduring equilibrium and the long-term consolidation of President Museveni's rule can be attributed to a distinctive form of governance: civil authoritarianism. This hybrid authoritarianism integrates centralized military authority with strategic accommodation of societal actors such as religious institutions, traditional monarchies, landed elites, and legacy political parties. It privileges regime survival and political order while maintaining selective responsiveness to entrenched social forces.

I advance two core arguments. First, although the NRA secured a decisive military victory in 1986, it inherited a *residual social structure*—a constellation of deeply rooted social actors that had endured through decades of conflict and upheaval. Rather than dismantling these actors through brute force, the NRM was compelled to negotiate with, co-opt, and accommodate them. This approach gave rise to a form of civil authoritarianism specifically calibrated to incorporate and manage their divergent interests.

Second, Museveni's government has found that exclusive reliance on coercion is both politically risky and costly to its legitimacy. In response, the regime has adopted a hybrid strategy that combines conventional state violence with more subtle instruments of control—most notably co-optation, selective accommodation, and delegated violence. While repression remains central, it is recurrently outsourced to informal or quasi-state actors such as the Kiboko Squad, the Kalangala Action Plan, and Crime Preventers. These groups function as key instruments for sustaining regime dominance while preserving the façade of civilian rule and enabling plausible deniability.

This dual logic—of embedded social negotiation and repression—distinguishes Uganda's authoritarian model from more overtly coercive regimes, such as that of President Paul Kagame in Rwanda. Kagame's administration employs highly centralized, bureaucratized, and overt violence as a governance tool. In contrast, Museveni's regime prefers institutional ambiguity and informal enforcement, allowing coercion to coexist with managed participation.

I conceptualize civil authoritarianism as a distinct variant of authoritarian governance characterized by the centralization of political authority in the hands of a dominant leader or a narrow ruling elite, alongside the selective incorporation of societal actors. Unlike autocracy or militarized authoritarian systems, civil authoritarian regimes preserve constrained civic and institutional spaces—allowing religious institutions, traditional authorities, landed elites, and legacy political movements to engage with the state on negotiated terms. This model facilitates regime stability not solely through overt repression but through a calibrated blend of coercion, co-optation, and strategic accommodation. Civil authoritarianism thus reflects an adaptive mode of rule in which political control is embedded within localized networks of legitimacy and influence, enabling authoritarian consolidation under the guise of civilian governance. In Uganda, for example, Museveni has centralized executive authority, curtailed civil liberties, and restricted civic space. Yet entrenched social groups continue to operate within this limited arena, retaining residual legitimacy and negotiating capacity. Their bounded autonomy allows them to shape state behavior in subtle but significant ways. This synthesis of executive dominance and selective societal accommodation forms the foundation of the NRM's durable civil authoritarianism.

A Contextual Overview of Residual Social Structures

Scholarship on authoritarian durability highlights regimes strategic deployment of co-optation, repression, censorship, propaganda, and institutional manipulation to consolidate power.[33] A prominent strand of literature emphasizes how formal institutions distribute patronage to co-opt elites and reinforce regime resilience.[34] Others focus on the containment of elite defection and integration of potential rivals—especially influential societal actors—into the architecture of rule.[35] These tactics range from legalizing constrained opposition and forging power-sharing arrangements, to recognizing religious and traditional authorities, restricting the media and civil society organisations, and staging sham elections.[36] More recently, the literature on political settlements has highlighted the distribution of power among elites and social actors in both democratic and authoritarian contexts, and how this distribution shapes institutional development, policy trajectories, and post-conflict outcomes.

In Uganda, four decades into NRM rule, the regime's relationship with entrenched societal actors—i.e., monarchies, churches, landed elites, remains contentious, strategic, and revealing.[37] Despite its authoritarian nature, Museveni's regime has consistently sought accommodation rather than outright marginalization. As Rabecca Tapscott observes, Museveni presides over "modern authoritarianism," where arbitrary power is layered with fragmented authority—permitting certain actors to wield constrained but meaningful influence.[38] Similarly, Golooba-Mutebi and Hickey (2013) describe NRM governance as an elite bargain that stabilizes the sociopolitical order through pragmatic incorporation.[39]

This book introduces the concept of *residual social structure* to refer to deeply embedded societal groups that survived Uganda's civil war and continue to shape post-conflict politics. These actors, including monarchies, churches, landed elites, and historic political parties, not only predate NRM rule but also persist as autonomous agents whose legitimacy, institutional memory, and collective interests must be managed rather than rejected. They challenge regime hegemony not through direct opposition alone, but by negotiating the terms of political inclusion. Existing scholarship rarely foregrounds this social inheritance, focusing instead on formal institutions or elite coalitions. This book addresses this gap by demonstrating how Uganda's residual social structure constrains authoritarian consolidation and subtly influences the exercise of power.

Three core attributes define these residual social actors. First, they possess informal veto power over select regime decisions. Second, they exhibit historical continuity, collective identity, and sociopolitical relevance despite efforts at marginalization. Third, they maintain organizational coherence and actively pursue strategic interests. The Buganda Kingdom, Anglican and Catholic churches, landed elites, and legacy parties such as the Democratic Party (DP) and Uganda People's Congress (UPC) exemplify these traits.

The NRM regime has responded not by seeking to dismantle these groups, but with calibrated engagement through co-optation, selective repression, and symbolic accommodation. This relationship is reciprocal and dynamic. Residual actors, though outside formal state institutions, have periodically compelled regime recalibration. Simultaneously, the regime draws on these actors' embedded networks to legitimate its authority. This symbiosis allows entrenched groups to extract concessions while the regime fortifies its political architecture. The endurance of these actors tempers Museveni's reliance on brute coercion, producing a distinct form of civil authoritarianism—a regime type negotiated through embedded societal forces rather than coercion imposed from above.

By instrumentalizing residual social structures, the NRM has mitigated elite fragmentation and pre-empted large-scale social mobilization against the regime. Uganda's authoritarian order is thus upheld not by absolute repression, but through controlled pluralism, tactical inclusion, and fragmented dissent. Selective tolerance enables certain actors to shape public discourse, while legal constraints and institutional ambiguity weaken collective opposition. Ultimately, residual social structures remain active but constrained, operating within boundaries narrowly defined by the regime.

Summary of the Chapters

The eight substantive chapters of this book are organized into two parts. Part one traces the foundations of NRM rule, conceptualizes the "residual social structure," and explains the NRA's dual strategy of coercion and co-optation. A central theme is the constraining influence of entrenched social groups on the regime's use of violence. The NRA's survival and eventual entrenchment in power were facilitated by its pragmatic accommodation of former rebel factions, the incorporation of potential adversaries into state structures, and the selective use of repression against non-compliant actors. This section also foregrounds the social-structural foundations of postcolonial Uganda, highlighting the persistence of entrenched class divisions, monarchism, and religious cleavages that complicated state formation. A key conclusion is that these social groups are not passive remnants of a precolonial or colonial past, but active political agents that have significantly shaped Uganda's postwar political order.

The second part focuses on the coercive strategies the NRM has deployed to contain entrenched social groups and political opposition seeking to challenge its authority. The chapters in this section examine the institutional architecture established by the NRA after the 1986 civil war—particularly the strategic design and instrumental use of the army, police, and intelligence agencies for regime survival. Once consolidated in power, the NRM used the security apparatus to suppress anti-regime mobilization, curb the influence of entrenched social groups, and stifle dissent within its own ranks. A central theme is that the regime has not sought to eradicate the opposition or dismantle residual social structures entirely. Instead, it has pursued a containment strategy that undermines rivals' capacity for collective action and confines their activities to localized, fragmented efforts posing minimal threat to regime stability. Moreover, domestic and international pressure over the regime's coercive actions has forced the NRM regime to blend formal state coercion with informal non-state coercive actors, preserving a degree of deniability and evading accountability. As a result, vigilante groups have played an instrumental role in consolidating and extending the NRM's power, with implications for the state's monopoly over legitimate force.

Part One of the book begins with Chapter 1, which serves as an introduction examining the historical crises that have shaped the post-independence Ugandan state and, more broadly, the African state. It introduces the central concept of the *residual social structure*—entrenched social formations that both predate and survive episodes of state collapse and civil war. The chapter also engages key debates on postcolonial African state formation, portraying postwar state development as a complex and contested process, shaped by intersecting historical, institutional, and social forces.

Chapter 2 examines the emergence of the NRM regime in Uganda, tracing its ascent to power and unpacking the historical and institutional foundations of what I define as *civil authoritarianism*. The chapter advances three central arguments. First, the success of the NRA as a guerrilla movement stemmed from its coherent ideological orientation and robust organizational structure, both cultivated and disseminated by the elite leadership at the helm of the NRM. Second, while the NRA secured a decisive military victory, it did not rely exclusively on coercion to consolidate authority. Instead, it acknowledged the limitations of violence and employed a blend of coercive and non-coercive strategies to establish legitimacy within the complex terrain of postwar governance. Third, I contend that Uganda's state reconstruction produced a civil-authoritarian mode of rule—one shaped not only by the NRA's coercive and ideological imperatives but also by enduring social structures that predated the NRM's rise.

Chapter 3 examines how the NRA, upon seizing power in 1986, navigated Uganda's fractured post-conflict landscape marked by competing armed groups, ethnic militias, and remnants of the former regime's security forces. While the chapter focuses on the neutralization of armed rivals, it argues that the NRA pursued a dual strategy of coercion and co-optation that enabled the consolidation of power in a volatile environment. On the one hand, the regime launched military offensives and intelligence operations to dismantle insurgent networks that posed immediate threats—particularly in the north and northeast. On the other hand, it selectively co-opted former rebel factions, offering them positions in the army, government, or local administration in exchange for loyalty. Groups such as NLF were absorbed through peace deals and integration into the national army, while others were neutralized through military repression. The chapter underscores how this strategy of calibrated violence and accommodation allowed the NRM to simultaneously pacify the security landscape, expand its political coalition, and prevent the emergence of a unified armed insurgency. Ultimately, these tactics underpinned the regime's survival, consolidation, and transformation into a dominant post-conflict political force.

Chapter 4 interrogates the interplay between Uganda's residual social structures and post-1986 state formation under the National Resistance Movement (NRM). It foregrounds the limitations of coercive control and explores the strategic bargains that have facilitated the consolidation of authoritarian rule. The chapter argues that the NRM's capacity to govern and maintain stability has hinged not merely on military dominance, but on its ability to negotiate with, accommodate, and selectively incorporate entrenched social forces into the postwar political order. These forces—including monarchies, religious institutions, landed elites, and urban business actors—are not passive relics of the past, but enduring power centers whose cooperation remains vital to regime durability. The NRM's political survival has depended on its skillful management of these actors' competing interests through strategic balancing, transforming potential sources of resistance into conditional allies. Ultimately, the chapter contends that the resilience of Uganda's authoritarian regime lies not in coercion alone, but in its adaptive engagement with historically embedded social structures.

Part two of the book opens with Chapter 5, which examines three interrelated dynamics that underscore the instrumental role of the military in sustaining the NRM regime: the personalization of the army, the transformation of the Uganda People's Defence Forces (UPDF) into a closed institutional domain governed by kinship, loyalty, and familial ties, and the systematic marginalization of ambitious officers perceived as potential rivals. From the early years of NRM rule, President Museveni prioritized the construction of a loyal and ideologically aligned military elite, positioning himself as both Commander-in-Chief and the ultimate arbiter of military appointments, promotions, and deployments. Over time, this control evolved into a deeply personalized system in which trust, ethnic affiliation, and familial proximity to the president—rather than merit or seniority—became key determinants of advancement within the UPDF. The creation and elevation of elite military units such as the Presidential Protection Unit (PPU), later renamed the Presidential Protection Brigade (PGB) and afterwards Special Forces Command (SFC), exemplify this dynamic. These units are staffed predominantly by officers from Museveni's inner circle and are often led by his close relatives, most notably his son, Gen. Muhoozi Kainerugaba. This has allowed Museveni to ring-fence core security functions within a tightly controlled family-dominated structure, thereby curbing contestation within the armed forces that could threaten regime durability. Collectively, these practices have transformed the UPDF into a politicized and personalized apparatus of regime security. The result is a military that functions more as a vertically integrated pillar of authoritarian rule—loyal not to the republic, but to the person of President Museveni.

Following the personalization of the military, the NRM strategically deployed the UPDF and broader security apparatus to neutralize internal threats, deter coups, and ensure the long-term survival of the regime. Chapter 6 explores how this securitized logic of regime protection has been actualized, focusing on the coordinated roles of the army, police, and intelligence agencies. These institutions have been instrumental not only in suppressing external opposition, but also in surveillant, disciplining, and stifling dissent within the regime's own ranks. The chapter argues that, despite its authoritarian nature, the NRM has not pursued a strategy of total annihilation of political opposition or residual social structures. Instead, it has relied on a more sophisticated logic of containment, one that seeks to disrupt adversaries' capacity for collective action, fragment their organizational coherence, and co-opt or intimidate key leaders. This strategy limits dissent to isolated, localized, and ultimately manageable expressions that do not pose a systemic threat to regime durability. Rather than eliminating the opposition and errant social groups outrightly, the NRM's approach has been to weaken their institutional strength and prevent horizontal linkages that could catalyze coordinated resistance. By delegitimizing, dividing, and containing potential challengers while maintaining a façade of pluralism, the regime has maintained tight control over the political field without relying exclusively on overt repression. Ultimately, the chapter contends that this strategy of controlled fragmentation has enabled the NRM to manage dissent without provoking large-scale anti-regime mobilisation, thus reinforcing the durability of its authoritarian order.

Chapter 7 examines the NRM regime's covert use of violence through three informal, non-state actors in Uganda—the Kiboko Squad, the Crime Preventers, and the Kalangala Action Plan. It explains why the regime tolerates, encourages, and, in some cases, orchestrates third-party violence against political opponents, despite the continued functionality of formal state coercive institutions. The chapter argues that the regime increasingly relies on these proxy actors to deploy violence in ways that shield it from direct accountability and reduce the risk of backlash from entrenched social groups. As a result, vigilante groups have become instrumental in consolidating and extending NRM's political dominance. The chapter further interrogates the strategic logic behind this outsourced violence and its broader implications for the state's monopoly on the legitimate use of force.

Chapter 8 concludes the study by offering key reflections on the findings, outlining their broader implications for understanding authoritarian durability in post-conflict states, and considering the possible future trajectories of the NRM regime. It synthesizes the core arguments developed throughout the book, emphasizing how the interplay between militarization, elite co-optation, and the strategic management of residual social structures has enabled the NRM to consolidate and sustain authoritarian rule over time. The chapter also reflects on the limits of this model, particularly in light of growing intra-elite tensions, generational shifts, and the uncertainties surrounding political succession. Taken together, these reflections contribute to a deeper understanding of how post-conflict authoritarian regimes adapt, endure, and potentially unravel.

Notes

1. Karugire, S. R. (1980). *A political history of Uganda*. Heinemann Educational Books.
2. Kiyimba, A. (1998). [Rev. of *The Ghost of Idi Amin in Ugandan Literature*]. *Research in African Literatures*, *29*(1), 124–138.
3. Rummel, R. J., & Horowitz, I. L. (1994). *Death by Government* (1st ed., pp. xxiii–xxiii). Routledge. https://doi.org/10.4324/9780203793756.
4. Thomas, C. (2022). Uganda–Tanzania War. In *Oxford Research Encyclopedia of African History*. Oxford University Press. https://doi.org/10.1093/acrefore/9780190277734.013.1040.
5. Meert, A. (2020). Suffering, Consent, and Coercion in Uganda: The Luwero War, 1981–1986. *The International Journal of African Historical Studies*, *53*(3), 389.
6. Willis, J., Lynch, G., & Cheeseman, N. (2017). "A valid electoral exercise"? Uganda's 1980 Elections and the Observers' Dilemma. *Comparative Studies in Society and History*, *59*(1), 211–238. https://doi.org/10.1017/S001041751600058X.
7. Turner, B. (2003). Uganda: Republic of Uganda. In *The Statesman's Yearbook* (pp. 1606–1611). Palgrave Macmillan UK. https://doi.org/10.1057/9780230271326_284.
8. Ciment, J. (1999). Uganda: Civil Conflict Since 1980. In *Encyclopedia of Conflicts Since World War II* (1st ed., pp. 1233–1237). Routledge. https://doi.org/10.4324/9780203058664-175.
9. Stapleton, T. (2018). Post-colonial civil wars (1955–2000). In *Africa: War and Conflict in the Twentieth Century* (1st ed., Vol. 1, pp. 87–111). Routledge. https://doi.org/10.4324/9781351104685-5.
10. Lidow, N. H. (2016). *Violent order: understanding rebel governance through Liberia's civil war*. Cambridge University Press.
11. Kelsall T. (2004). *Between democracy and terror: the Sierra Leone civil war*. Council for the Development of Social Science Research in Africa.
12. Temesgen Duressa, G., Ta'a, T., & Debu, D. (2024). The Marxist concept of national question and the analysis of Ethiopian reality during the Derg regime (1974 to 1991). *Cogent Arts & Humanities*, *11*(1). https://doi.org/10.1080/23311983.2024.2347056.

13. Lyons, T. (2021). The Origins of the EPRDF and the Prospects for the Prosperity Party. *Journal of Asian and African Studies (Leiden)*, *56*(5), 1051–1063. https://doi.org/10.1177/00219096211007658.
14. Soderlund, W. C., & Briggs, E. D. (2014). Sudan's North–South Divide. In *The Independence of South Sudan* (pp. 1–12). Wilfrid Laurier University Press. https://doi.org/10.51644/9781771120838-003.
15. Adekanye, J. (1996). Rwanda/Burundi: "Uni-ethnic" Dominance and the Cycle of Armed Ethnic Formations. *Social Identities*, *2*(1), 37–72. https://doi.org/10.1080/13504639652385.
16. Sandbrook, R., & Barker, J. (2011). *Politics of Africa's Economic Stagnation* (1st ed.). Cambridge University Press.
17. Tripp, A. M. (2004). The Changing Face of Authoritarianism in Africa: The Case of Uganda. *Africa Today*, *50*(3), 3–26. https://doi.org/10.1353/at.2004.0035.
18. Paine, J. (2019). Ethnic Violence in Africa: Destructive Legacies of Pre-Colonial States. *International Organization*, *73*(3), 645–683. https://doi.org/10.1017/S0020818319000134.
19. Ito, G. (2021). Why does ethnic partition foster violence? Unpacking the deep historical roots of civil conflicts. *Journal of Peace Research*, *58*(5), 986–1003. https://doi.org/10.1177/0022343320957377.
20. Migdal, J. S. (1988). *Strong Societies and Weak States: State-Society Relations and State Capabilities in the Third World*. Princeton University Press.
21. Wubneh, M. (2015). This land is my land: the Ethio-Sudan boundary and the need to rectify arbitrary colonial boundaries. *Journal of Contemporary African Studies*, *33*(4), 441–466.
22. Chabal, P., & Daloz, JP (1999). *Africa Works*. Disorder as Political Instrument. Oxford: James Curry.
23. Young, C. (2012). *The postcolonial state in Africa: fifty years of independence, 1960–2010*. The University of Wisconsin Press.
24. Young, C. (2012) ibid.
25. Joseph, R. A. (1999). *State, conflict, and democracy in Africa*. L. Rienner.
26. Moreno-Torres, M. & Anderson, M. (2004) Fragile States: Defining Difficult Environments for Poverty Reduction. *Department for International Development (DFID)*, United Kingdom.

27. Young, C. (1994). *The African colonial state in comparative perspective*. Yale University Press.
28. Helman, G. B., & Ratner, S. R. (1992). Saving Failed States. Foreign Policy, 89, 3–20. https://doi.org/10.2307/1149070.
29. Onslow, S. (2009). *Cold war in southern Africa: white power, black liberation* (1st ed.). Routledge.
30. Beiruti, A. (2020). *The Cold War Congo: The Congo Crisis and the Primary Determinants of US Cold War Foreign Policy (1952–1964)*. ProQuest Dissertations & Theses.
31. Harshé, R. (2019). *Africa in world affairs: politics of imperialism, the Cold War and globalization*. Routledge.
32. Mazov, S. V. (2010). *A distant front in the Cold War: the USSR in West Africa and Congo, 1956-1964*. Woodrow Wilson Center Press.
33. Little, Andrew T. (2017) "Propaganda and Credulity." Games and Economic Behavior102: 224–32; Edmond, Chris. 2013. "Information Manipulation, Coordination, and Regime Change." Review of Economic Studies 80: 1422–58.10.1093; Rozenas, Arturas, and Stukal, Denis (2019) "How Autocrats Manipulate Economic News: Evidence from Russia's State-Controlled Television." Journal of Politics 81: 982–96.
34. Gandhi, J. 2010. *Political institutions under dictatorship*. Cambridge University Press; Tsourapas, G. 2021. "Global Autocracies: Strategies of Transnational Repression, Legitimation, and Co-Optation in World Politics." *International Studies Review*, *23*(3), 616–644.
35. Slater, D. (2010) *Ordering Power: Contentious Politics and Authoritarian Leviathans in Southeast Asia*. Cambridge University Press; Gandhi, J., & Przeworski, A. (2007). Authoritarian Institutions and the Survival of Autocrats. *Comparative Political Studies*, *40*(11), 1279–1301; Svolik M.W. The Politics of Authoritarian Rule. Cambridge University Press; 2012.
36. Levitsky, S., & Way, L. A (2010) *Competitive Authoritarianism: Hybrid Regimes After the Cold War*. Cambridge, UK: Cambridge University Press; Magaloni B. 2006. *Voting for Autocracy: Hegemonic Party Survival and Its Demise in Mexico*. Cambridge University Press; 2006; Bellin, E. 2004. The Robustness of Authoritarianism in the Middle East: Exceptionalism in Comparative Perspective. *Comparative Politics*, *36*(2), 139–157.

37. Kiyimba, K. 2017. An Analysis of the Epistemic Link between the Catholic Religion and Violence in Uganda's History. *Journal for the Study of Religion*, *30*(1), 26–51.
38. Tapscott, R., & Ebscohost E-Books—York University. (2021). Arbitrary states: social control and modern authoritarianism in Museveni's Uganda (First edition) Oxford University Press.
39. Golooba-Mutebi, F. and Hickey. S. (2013). Investigating the Links between Political Settlements and Inclusive Development in Uganda: Towards a Research Agenda. *ESID Working Paper* No. 20, Manchester: University of Manchester.

CHAPTER 2

Building Power from the Periphery: The Rise and Consolidation of the NRM Regime

The excitement and jubilation that followed Idi Amin's 1971 coup were short-lived. He had promised a swift return to democracy but instead went about murdering his critics, including the Archbishop of Kampala and the Chief Justice.[1] Amin presided over an eight-year period of economic collapse, extrajudicial killings, torture and dispossession of multitudes that left the country pauperized.[2] The initial public euphoria that greeted his rise to power quickly dissipated as his regime became synonymous with repression and brutality. Over the course of eight years, Amin presided over the collapse of Uganda's economy and plunged much of the population into severe poverty. He was eventually overthrown in 1979 by a coalition of Ugandan exiles supported by Tanzanian forces, bringing an end to one of the most violent dictatorships in post-colonial Africa.

In the aftermath of Amin's fall, national elections were held in 1980, which resulted in Obote's return to power.[3] However, Obote's second administration proved no less repressive than his first. His regime relied heavily on state terror, exacerbating economic decline and fostering pervasive insecurity. Mounting discontent led to the emergence of numerous armed insurgencies. In July 1985, Obote was ousted in yet another military coup, this time orchestrated by Brigadier Basilio Olara Okello.[4]

G. Bareebe, *Social Structures and the Making of Museveni's Civil-Authoritarian Regime in Uganda*,
https://doi.org/10.1007/978-3-032-14015-9_2

The July 1985 coup marked a critical turning point in Uganda's post-independence political crisis. It ushered in a brief, but turbulent period marked by deepening political instability, economic collapse, and intensifying ethnic tensions within both the military and broader society. Lacking political legitimacy and a clear governing strategy, the new military junta struggled to assert effective control, further weakening state authority and exacerbating internal divisions. Amid this climate of uncertainty and political fragmentation, the NRA capitalized on the regime's disarray—expanding its territorial reach, consolidating popular support, and presenting itself as a more disciplined and politically viable alternative. These developments laid the groundwork for the NRA's final military offensives, culminating in the capture of Kampala and the seizure of state power in January 1986.

The chapter begins with a historical overview of the National Resistance Army, the guerrilla force that overthrew the regimes of Milton Obote and later Tito Okello Lutwa and captured power in 1986. By tracing the historical roots and strategic choices of the NRA during the post-war reconstruction period, this chapter highlights the complex interplay between military victory, ideological framing, and existing social structure in shaping state formation. Uganda's experience shows that insurgent movements, when successful, must grapple not only with the legacies of war but also with the constraints and possibilities embedded in pre-existing political and social order.

The Origins and Organization of the NRA/NRM

In the early 1980s, the NRA, a guerrilla movement led by Yoweri Museveni, emerged from the rural hinterlands of central Uganda as a formidable insurgent force.[5] In the aftermath of the contested 1980 elections, which returned Milton Obote to power amidst widespread allegations of electoral fraud, Museveni and a number of opposition groups declared war on the reinstated Obote regime. While the government quickly neutralized most rival insurgencies, the NRA demonstrated a remarkable capacity for resilience, organization, and tactical adaptation, ultimately prevailing over state forces.

A key factor in the NRA's durability was its operational base in the Luwero Triangle, a rural region deeply alienated from the central government. This territorial positioning provided both a strategic advantage and harbour for the rebellion. The Baganda's hostility toward Obote's regime enabled the NRA to recruit from local peasant communities, secure logistical support, and embed itself within a population that viewed the state as predatory and illegitimate. The NRA's grassroots mobilization efforts were underpinned by a deliberate effort to frame the rebellion as a national liberation struggle, rather than an ethnically or regionally narrow insurgency. Important to the NRA's success was its organizational adaptability and inclusive approach to alliance-building. Unlike other insurgent groups that pursued narrow agendas or operated in isolation, the NRA actively sought to integrate other armed factions opposing the Obote government. This strategy of coalition-building was both pragmatic and ideological and allowed the NRA to organically develop its fighting capacity while reinforcing its claim to national legitimacy. Among the groups co-opted into the NRA's ranks were the Uganda National Army (UNA), comprised largely of former soldiers from Idi Amin's regime, and two Baganda-dominated movements—the Uganda Freedom Movement (UFM) and the Federal Democratic Movement of Uganda (FEDEMU).[6] This incorporation of rival militias was not without challenges, particularly given the divergent backgrounds and political orientations of the constituent groups. However, the NRA leadership maintained a central command structure that emphasized political education, ideological discipline, and internal cohesion. These features helped prevent factionalism and enabled the NRA to project itself not merely as a military force, but also as the nucleus of a future governing authority.

The ideological foundations that shaped Museveni's decision to form a guerrilla movement can be traced to the political crises that engulfed Uganda in the 1960s and 1970s. These formative decades were marked by constitutional instability, authoritarian consolidation, and violent repression, all of which informed Museveni's vision that would later guide the NRA. The ideological framework developed during this period became integral not only to the internal organizational structure of the NRA, but also to the social-psychological orientation of its leadership. As the principal architect of the NRA's vision, Museveni maintained that Uganda's political stability was attainable only through a radical socio-political transformation—one rooted in the strategy of a protracted people's war.

Museveni's conception of armed struggle drew heavily from Marxist-Leninist thought, anti-colonial liberation ideologies, and his personal experiences with revolutionary movements elsewhere on the continent. His exposure to the Front for the Liberation of Mozambique (FRELIMO) under the leadership of Samora Machel played a decisive role in shaping his strategic thinking. [7] FRELIMO's successful insurgency against Portuguese colonial rule illustrated that an armed movement, grounded in peasant mobilization and political education, could build strength gradually and overturn systemic oppression, even when starting from a position of strategic weakness.[8] Museveni leveraged his personal relationship with Machel to undergo specialized military training in Mozambique, and he facilitated similar training for key NRA founders, including Fred Rwigema and Salim Saleh (Museveni's half-brother). [9] These experiences laid the technical and ideological groundwork for the creation of a disciplined guerrilla force.

Museveni has frequently cited 1966—the year then-Prime Minister Milton Obote abrogated the 1962 independence constitution—as a turning point in his political consciousness. At the time, Museveni was a student at Ntare School, a prestigious boys' secondary school in western Uganda. The abrogation of the constitution and the subsequent Kabaka Crisis, in which Obote ordered a military assault on the Buganda kingdom, crystallized Museveni's belief in the necessity of armed resistance.[10] The enactment of the 1967 Republican Constitution, which abolished traditional kingdoms and centralized power under Obote, further entrenched authoritarian rule and set the stage for the country's descent into political violence and instability. For Museveni, these developments confirmed that reform from within the existing state structure was impossible. Instead, a revolutionary transformation, anchored in long-term armed struggle and popular mobilization, was essential. The NRA, therefore, emerged not only as a military response to the Obote regime, but as the institutional embodiment of a broader ideological project that linked Uganda's contemporary crisis to the failures of post-independence governance.[11]

Accordingly, President Museveni's journey to launching an armed rebellion was shaped not only by Uganda's post-independence political crises but also by formative transnational experiences during his education and exile. After completing secondary school in Uganda, Museveni pursued higher education in Tanzania, a country that had become a hub for African liberation movements. There, he encountered prominent figures such as Eduardo Mondlane, the founding president of FRELIMO, Mozambique's anti-colonial movement.[12] According to Museveni's own wartime memoir, he exchanged ideas with Mondlane on the strategic and organizational challenges of confronting entrenched regimes. These interactions deepened Museveni's conviction in the efficacy of rural-based insurgency and in the transformative power of protracted armed struggle.[13]

FRELIMO's strategy of mobilizing peasants and operating from liberated rural zones made a lasting impression on Museveni. After visiting FRELIMO-controlled areas, he came to believe that war, far from being merely destructive, could play a redemptive role in political education and in emancipating the peasantry from "parochial identities and a colonial mindset."[14] These insights would become central to the ideological orientation of the NRA, which later presented itself as a people's movement—one grounded in the interests of ordinary Ugandans and committed to national liberation through sustained grassroots mobilization.[15]

Upon returning to Uganda, Museveni's plans for political transformation were interrupted by Amin's 1971 coup, which forced him into exile in Tanzania. While in Tanzania, he became a founding member of the Front for National Salvation (FRONASA), a rebel group aiming to depose Amin. Museveni attempted to push the FRELIMO model within FRONASA, advocating for guerrilla warfare and political indoctrination. [16] However, these views met resistance from other members who favored a swift, conventional military campaign.[17] The strategic and ideological disagreements, compounded by early military failures, led to the inactivity of FRONASA between 1973 and 1976.[18]

Museveni used this lull to deepen his ties with FRELIMO, which had successfully ousted Portuguese colonial rule in Mozambique. He sent 26 combatants for guerrilla training in FRELIMO camps—many of whom would later become pivotal in reviving FRONASA and forming the core leadership of the NRA. This period of consolidation proved instrumental when the geopolitical tide turned. Amin's 1978 invasion of Tanzania's Kagera region provoked a full-scale military response from the Tanzanian army, which, with FRONASA's support, overthrew Amin in 1979.[19] Museveni emerged as a key political actor in the transitional government—serving as Vice Chair of the Presidential Commission and Minister for Regional Cooperation.[20] Yet the return to civilian rule was short-lived. The 1980 general elections, which many Ugandans hoped would mark a democratic turning point, were widely perceived as fraudulent. Museveni had by then formed the Uganda Patriotic Movement (UPM) political party and stood as its presidential flagbearer. The entire electoral process—from constituency demarcation to vote tabulation—was controlled by the ruling Uganda People's Congress (UPC).[21] Acting head of state Paulo Muwanga issued a decree mandating that all election results be submitted to him personally, effectively rendering the Electoral Commission powerless. Days later, Muwanga unilaterally declared Obote the winner. In a move that revealed the transactional nature of this arrangement, Obote reappointed Muwanga as his deputy and Minister of Defense.

Museveni rejected both the legitimacy of the elections and the resulting regime. During the campaign period, he had warned that electoral manipulation would be met with force, vowing to respond to "intimidation with intimidation, violence with violence."[22] For Museveni, the 1980 elections confirmed his belief that Uganda's political elite—entrenched through a legacy of ethnic manipulation and militarized patronage—could not be dislodged through electoral means.[23] He maintained that true democratization required not only regime change but the dismantling of the socio-political architecture that sustained elite dominance. This conviction formed the intellectual and strategic basis for launching a new armed struggle.

In January 1981, Museveni initiated a guerrilla movement that would evolve into the NRA. Unlike earlier insurgencies, the NRA was informed by a coherent ideological vision and an expansive organizational strategy shaped by lessons from African liberation movements. It aimed not merely at regime overthrow but at building a new political order based on inclusion, discipline, and grassroots mobilization. In this sense, the NRA represented the culmination of Museveni's long-held belief in the necessity of an armed struggle as a vehicle for political transformation in Uganda.

The Transformation of NRA from Guerrilla Force to National Army

The NRA publicly declared its existence on February 6, 1981, with a surprise assault on the Kabamba military barracks in central Uganda's Mubende District.[24] Though the operation failed, the attack marked the beginning of the NRA sustained guerrilla insurgency. The choice of Kabamba as the NRA's first target was strategic. First, the barracks housed a substantial stockpile of weapons, which the NRA hoped to seize to aid a broader rebellion. Second, Kabamba's remote location offered operational advantages as government reinforcements would be delayed, thereby increasing the chances of a successful raid. Third, by striking a national military installation, the NRA intended to assert dominance over rival rebel factions—such as Kikosi-Vita, the Uganda Freedom Movement (UFM), and the so-called "Communist Group"—and establish itself as the vanguard of the anti-government resistance.[25]

However, the Kabamba raid did not unfold as planned. Tanzanian troops stationed at the barracks repelled the attack, forcing the NRA fighters to retreat with only a few weapons. The failed operation demoralized many in Museveni's ranks and provoked frustration among rival factions, especially those awaiting arms shipments from Libya. Leaders such as Andrew Kayiira and Yusuf Lule accused Museveni of jeopardizing their operations by triggering a government crackdown that included roadblocks, disrupting arms deliveries. Fred Guweddeko, a former NRA commanding officer in charge of operations explains:

> They did not want any insecurity to jeopardize the delivery of the guns. Any chaos would cause the UNLA to set up roadblocks. Kayiira had already received some arms and was waiting for another consignment.[26]

Despite the setback, Museveni pressed ahead with his vision of unifying the fragmented resistance. Though he had a strained relationship with Libyan leader Muammar Gaddafi—stemming from Museveni's prior alignment with Israel during the campaign against Gaddafi-backed Amin—he still sought to integrate groups that had Gaddafi's support.[27] Over time, many joined Museveni's effort, enabling the NRA to grow in size and strength. Its expansion was not simply military but also political as the NRA gained legitimacy and manpower by assimilating other rebel factions that shared its goal of ousting Milton Obote's regime.

After retreating into the Luwero Triangle, the NRA established de facto control over significant territory in central Uganda. There, it created safe zones, established training camps, recruited combatants, and built rudimentary governance structures.[28] The NRA raided villages for food and labor and launched sporadic ambushes on government forces.[29] By late 1982, it was evident that the state no longer held a monopoly on violence. The Uganda National Liberation Army (UNLA), the national army loyal to Obote, responded with a brutal counterinsurgency campaign, marked by mass killings and civilian repression. The NRA survived by relocating deeper into rural areas such as Singo, where it regrouped and intensified recruitment, including among disaffected youth and former UPC supporters fleeing the regime's violence.[30]

Following the 1985 coup by Gen. Tito Okello, there were brief hopes that the conflict would end. Peace negotiations were held in Nairobi, but hostilities resumed soon after, as both sides engaged in indiscriminate violence.[31] By early 1986, with a force estimated at 8,000 to 10,000 fighters, the NRA marched on Kampala and seized control, installing Museveni as head of a new government.[32]

Despite its origins as a rural insurgency, the NRA developed a sophisticated internal hierarchy. Museveni sat at the apex as commander-in-chief and exercised ultimate authority over strategic and operational matters.[33] He was supported by the High Command (HC), a dual organ that functioned both as a rank and a governing structure. The HC was composed primarily of educated elites, selected for their military experience, ideological commitment, or access to key networks and resources. Among the early HC members were Eriya Kategaya, Sam Magara, Elly Tumwine, Fred Rwigyema, Salim Saleh, David Tinyefuza, Matayo Kyaligonza, and Tadeo Kanyankole.

The HC functioned as the NRA's strategic brain trust. Promotion into this body conferred prestige, while demotion was regarded as disciplinary punishment, as in the case of Tinyefuza in 1984.[34] Beneath the HC was a broader group of Senior Officers forming the Defence Forces Council. These included figures like Chefe Ali, Pecos Kuteesa, Jim Muhwezi, Kahinda Otafiire, Ahmed Kashilingi, Ivan Koreta, Joram Mugume, and Mugisha Muntu, among others, who collectively formed the backbone of the guerrilla force.

By 1985, the NRA had incorporated a range of civilians—businesspeople, academics, professionals, and traditional leaders—into its ranks. These individuals, later referred to as the "NRA historicals," would become central to Uganda's post-conflict political and economic order. Parallel to the military structure, the NRA also maintained a political wing, the National Resistance Movement (NRM), headed by Museveni. The NRM included politicians, scholars, and exiles from the Obote regime, many of whom provided diplomatic support and strategic guidance from abroad.

Although the NRA presented itself as a peasant movement, grounded in rural struggle and popular grievances, the actual leadership and direction of the rebellion remained firmly in the hands of an educated and politically connected elite. The fusion of military and political organization enabled the NRA to function as both a guerrilla force and an embryonic state apparatus—laying the groundwork for a new order under Museveni's control.

Although Africa was widely perceived as economically impoverished, the bipolar world order of the 1980s transformed the continent into a geopolitical and geostrategic battleground between the communist bloc led by the USSR and the capitalist bloc led by the United States. Many of the era's civil wars in Africa were fought along ideological lines, as superpower rivalry enabled opportunistic post-independence leaders to secure modern weaponry, financial aid, and political backing. This patronage, often cynically exploited, prolonged and intensified conflicts in countries such as Zaire (now DRC), Ethiopia, Somalia, Angola, and Mozambique. Uganda's civil war, however, unfolded differently. Geostrategically peripheral, it failed to attract sustained interest from either Cold War camp. The NRA is therefore a rare case of a post-colonial African guerrilla movement that seized state power without the sponsorship of a major global power.

The absence of external patronage did not leave the NRA ideologically rudderless. On the contrary, Museveni and his close associates deliberately articulated what became known as the *bush war ideology*—a political-military doctrine that shaped both the conduct of the war and the organization of the movement. This ideology rested on three interrelated pillars. First, civilian participation: embedding the struggle within local communities to secure both material resources and moral support. Second, discipline: enforcing strict codes of conduct among combatants to distinguish the NRA from predatory armed groups and to cultivate popular trust. Third, sacrifice: fostering a collective ethos that placed the cause above personal gain, thereby reinforcing the movement's internal cohesion and legitimacy. The following section examines each of these pillars in detail.

Civilian Participation

From its inception, the NRA regarded civilian participation as essential to the success of guerrilla warfare. The movement took pride in establishing local administrative structures that would embed the struggle within the social fabric of rural communities.[35] Within just two years of its formation, the NRA introduced elections for village officials in territories under its control. Initially, these structures were clandestine, composed of village heads who formed a trusted network crucial for intelligence gathering, recruitment, and food provision for fighters. As the

NRA extended its territorial reach, this covert approach evolved into more open civilian participation, with village heads increasingly elected through popular vote.

The architects of this strategy worked from the premise that a participatory approach would secure grassroots legitimacy for the guerrillas, which could then be leveraged to mobilize broader resistance against the ruling government.[36] Drawing lessons from FRELIMO's experience in Mozambique, the NRA sought to frame civilian participation not merely as an operational necessity but as a political ideology in its own right.[37]

This approach set the NRA apart from many post-independence African insurgencies. Movements led by warlords—such as those in Liberia—made little effort to engage civilians in decision-making,[38] and others, like the Sudan People's Liberation Army (SPLA), relied more on coercion than persuasion to maintain cohesion.[39] Zimbabwe's African National Union (ZANU) likewise used force to mobilize peasants and compel compliance.[40] By contrast, the NRA attempted to integrate itself into civilian life by cultivating a network of local elites—elected through community processes—who served as intermediaries between guerrillas and the wider population. This was, in part, an effort to project the NRA as fundamentally different from the incumbent government, especially in matters of governance.[41]

The degree to which this participation was genuinely voluntary remains contested. While critics question whether civilians in NRA-controlled zones could truly make free choices without intimidation, many NRA veterans—including those now critical of Museveni—insist that the process was largely unmanipulated. According to one former NRA commander, the aim was to "give people a feel of democracy" and to demonstrate that the NRA offered a credible alternative to Obote's regime, which had discredited itself by rigging the 1980 elections.[42]

In theory, most guerrilla movements claim to win the "hearts and minds" of local populations, yet in practice, participation often blends persuasion with coercion.[43] The NRA was no exception. On several occasions, it used force to compel civilians to carry supplies, and it shelled certain civilian areas in ways that would inflame resentment against the government.[44] In other instances, its fighters looted farms and gardens, although there were also efforts to secure food voluntarily. Farmers were promised future compensation for their contributions, and the NRA kept detailed records of livestock and crops taken—whether voluntarily or by force—intending to repay these debts once in power.[45]

The deeper question is why the NRA's leadership invested so heavily in cultivating civilian participation. Two interpretations have since emerged: One views the exercise as primarily instrumental—a form of *siasa* (political propaganda) designed to convince rural populations that the guerrillas were genuinely committed to democracy, thereby mobilizing support and legitimizing their cause.[46] The other interpretation holds that the NRA was initially sincere in its democratic intentions but abandoned this commitment once in power, as Museveni moved to consolidate authority by outlawing political parties and narrowing political space. Under this view, the participatory structures of the bush war foreshadowed the "no-party" system of the first decade of Museveni's rule.[47] Even after the formal reintroduction of multiparty politics, the government tightly managed the electoral process, undermining the independence of Uganda's electoral institutions. As some critics have argued, "Museveni was more democratic when it served his interests in the bush; once in power, he became an authoritarian who organizes sham elections to legitimize his rule."[48]

Yet even during the bush war, NRA leaders were aware of the potential risks in fully opening political participation.[49] Some feared that elected local officials might not be reliable custodians of sensitive intelligence, leading to the creation of a parallel clandestine structure.[50] This second network—composed of trusted individuals selected through personal recommendation—operated alongside the elected committees. It consisted of respected elders, wealthy businessmen, politicians, cultural leaders, and church figures, many of whom had longstanding ties to the guerrillas.

Unlike the official elected committees, which functioned primarily in secure zones, clandestine committees operated in both NRA and government-controlled areas. They were critical in mobilizing resources, protecting guerrillas from informers, and gathering intelligence. The NRA's operational base in central Uganda, a region dominated by the Baganda—many of whom deeply resented Obote's rule—facilitated this work. The clandestine networks could operate in contested spaces and even behind enemy lines, where betrayal was more likely.

The existence of this dual structure reveals the NRA's pragmatic blend of participation and control. The official committees helped to cultivate a democratic image and channel civilian support, while the clandestine committees maintained tight control over sensitive operations and reduced the risk of infiltration. By managing information flow through trusted intermediaries, the NRA avoided what Norma Kriger describes as the "struggle within the struggle"[51]—i.e., the factional disputes and manipulation of local grievances that can destabilize insurgent movements. Moreover, by positioning themselves as arbiters in local disputes, the clandestine committees reinforced the NRA's role as both a protector and a political authority in the communities it sought to govern.[52]

Internal Discipline and Sacrifice

From both a political and military standpoint, senior NRA officers were initially concerned about the caliber and political orientation of new recruits. Many were considered amateurish, undisciplined, and potentially unreliable. To address this, the NRA deliberately worked to instill patriotism and a spirit of sacrifice by embedding fighters within the peasant communities they sought to liberate—and of which they considered themselves an integral part. Unlike many post-colonial African insurgencies that neglected ideological cohesion, the NRA believed that a politically illiterate and disorganized force posed a far greater internal challenge than one thoroughly politically oriented. Consequently, political education became a defining feature of both NRA ideology and practice. One senior NRA officer explains:

> We had studied most post-independence guerrilla groups in Africa. We made a departure because we realized that even fighters need a clear political ideology in order to succeed. Fighters need to understand why they are fighting and what they want from the war. That is precisely why, by the time we came to power, our fighters knew the kind of state we wanted to build.[53]

Accordingly, political orientation was central to improving combat effectiveness, enhancing discipline, and cultivating respect for civilian populations. Political mobilization was integrated into recruitment and training, with regular sessions conducted for both combatants and civilians to raise political consciousness and foster a shared vision.[54] The movement operated on the conviction that an informed understanding of the political context was indispensable for survival, legitimacy, and mobilization against Obote's regime. Reflecting this ethos, Museveni later remarked that he promoted political education among his fighters because "armies divorced from the people's interests habitually loot civilians" and that "conscious activists are necessary to arouse the masses."[55] The leaders in the NRA's political wing were likewise expected to visit the frontlines regularly to candidly experience the conditions of the "fighting masses" rather than remaining insulated from the struggle.[56]

Civilian support was especially vital given the NRA's lack of external backing. Neighboring regimes—most of them authoritarian—viewed the NRA insurgency as a destabilizing threat, fearing its success might embolden similar movements in their own territories.[57] This regional isolation forced the NRA to rely heavily on the peasantry in its controlled areas, who provided sanctuary and logistical support during intensified government offensives. In this context, discipline and respectful conduct toward civilians were not merely ideological commitments but a necessity for the movement's survival—marking a sharp contrast with other post-independence guerrilla forces that tolerated or encouraged predatory behavior.[58]

While the NRA, like all insurgent forces, engaged in violence during the conflict, the scale and character of its conduct differed significantly from that of its adversaries. In NRA-held territories, incidents of abuse were relatively rare, particularly when contrasted with the systematic brutality that characterized contested areas under government control. This restraint was partly a function of the NRA's geographically limited territorial base. Operating within a compact enclave meant that any misconduct risked rapidly undermining the movement's legitimacy and jeopardizing its survival. The leadership's physical and organizational proximity to both fighters and civilians facilitated tighter discipline, enabling the swift identification and suppression of criminal behavior, betrayal, or infiltration—an outcome far less achievable in larger, more territorially dispersed insurgencies.

To formalize relations between fighters and civilians, the NRA introduced a code of conduct in 1981. This outlined acceptable behavior not only toward civilians but also between combatants.[59] Severe offenses—including rape, murder, betrayal, and fatal insubordination—were punishable by death; lesser infractions were met with *kandoya*, a form of corporal punishment involving whipping and forced marches. Courts-martial were established in the bush, with each battalion maintaining its own judicial unit.[60] Civilians were invited to witness trials of soldiers accused of crimes against them, thereby enhancing transparency and reinforcing accountability.

One notable case occurred in 1982, when Zabroni, an intoxicated NRA soldier, was accused of killing villagers in Semuto. Despite appeals for leniency on grounds of intoxication, the high command approved his public execution.[61] Museveni justified this decision by invoking Mao Tse-tung's dictum: "never take a needle or thread from the people without paying for it."[62] Such public trials and punishments reinforced the perception of NRA fighters as disciplined and respectful compared to government troops, encouraging villagers and local elders to attend NRA meetings without fear.

At these gatherings, political cadres conducted ideological indoctrination sessions known locally as *Kipindi kya Siasa*. These aimed to instill perseverance, selflessness, and patriotism in both fighters and civilians. Certain areas, such as Kitemamasanga, became recognized centers of this political indoctrination. The program explicitly discouraged "pseudo-ideologies" based on ethnicity, nepotism, or chauvinism, promoting instead a nationalist and selfless ethos. Museveni consistently emphasized the need to transcend tribalism, religion, and male chauvinism, arguing that a capable army must be exemplary in conduct, well-trained, and ideologically conscious.[63] Importantly, the NRA framed its struggle as neither pro-capitalist nor pro-Marxist, rejecting the binary ideological alignments of the Cold War. Instead, it was presented as a civilian-led quest for socio-economic transformation, rooted in the consciousness and self-determination of the peasantry. As one officer reflected, the movement was "a product of a protracted people's struggle that strives for socio-economic transformation."[64]

The NRA's wartime emphasis on political education, discipline, and sacrifice did more than ensure military success. It forged the ideological and organizational blueprint for post-1986 governance. Internal cohesion, built on shared commitments and enforced by strict codes of conduct, translated into a governing style that blended centralized control with appeals to popular participation and order. This framework justified an emphasis on stability, disciplined administration, and rhetorical allegiance to peasant interests. Yet, the same mechanisms that fostered wartime unity—controlled participation, hierarchical oversight, and the suppression of dissent—also underpinned the civil-authoritarian nature of the NRM regime. In this way, the practices and ideology of the bush war were not abandoned after victory. They were institutionalized and shaped Uganda's political trajectory for decades.

Notes

1. Gwyn D., (1977) Idi Amin: death-light of Africa. Boston: *Little Brown.*
2. Furley O., (1989) Britain and Uganda from Amin to Museveni: Blind Eye Diplomacy. In: Kumar Rupesinghe (eds) *Conflict Resolution in Uganda,* Ohio University Press pp. 94–275.
3. Otunu O., (1987) *Politics and the military in Uganda.* 1890–1985, London, Macmillan Press.
4. Hansen H.B., (2013). Uganda in the 1970s: A Decade of Paradoxes and Ambiguities. *Journal of Eastern African Studies*, v.7 (1), p.83.
5. Makara S., Lakner L., et al. (2009) "Turnaround: The National Resistance Movement and the Reintroduction of a Multiparty System in Uganda" *International Political Science Review,* Vol. 30, No. 2, 185–204.
6. Interview with Shaban Bantariza, Uganda government deputy spokesperson. 18 June 2016.
7. Munslow B., (1985) (ed.), Samora M. *An African Revolutionary: Selected Speeches and Writings.* (London: Zed Pres.
8. Museveni Y.K., (2000) *What is Africa's Problem?* University of Minnesota Press; First edition.
9. Munslow B., (1985) ibid.
10. Goodfellow, T. & Lindemann, S. (2013). The clash of institutions: traditional authority, conflict and the failure of 'hybridity' in Buganda. *Commonwealth & Comparative politics* 5(1) pp. 3–26.
11. Oloka-Onyango, J. (1997). "The question of Buganda in contemporary Ugandan politics" *Journal of Contemporary African Studies*, 15(2), 173–189.
12. Museveni Y.K., (1997) *Sowing the Mustard seed: The struggle for freedom and democracy in Uganda.* Oxford: Macmillan.
13. Museveni Yoweri (1997) ibid. pp. 10–11.
14. Museveni Yoweri (1997) ibid.
15. Museveni Yoweri (1997) ibid. pp. 10–11.
16. Interview with Maj. John Kazoora, an NRA historical member (June 23, 2016).
17. Interview with Maj. John Kazoora. Ibid.
18. Museveni Yoweri (1997) ibid. 53–4.

19. Ivan S.G., (1980) *Ghosts of Kampala* Weidenfeld & Nicholson, London.
20. Acheson-Brown G. Daniel (2001) "The Tanzanian Invasion of Uganda: A Just War?" *International Third World Studies Journal* 121–11.
21. Okuku, J. (2003). Ethnicity, State Power and the Democratization Process in Uganda. *The Nordic Africa Institute. Discussion Paper* no. 17. Uppsala, Norway.
22. Weinstein J.M. (2006). *Inside Rebellion: The Politics of Insurgent Violence*. Cambridge University Press; 2006. p. 63.
23. Kategaya, E. (1990). Kategaya diagnoses Uganda's disease. In: *Mission to freedom: Uganda resistance news 1981–1985*, ed. James Tumusiime, 122–127. Kampala: *Directorate of Information and Mass Mobilisation*, NRM Secretariat.
24. Bratton, M. & Van de Walle N., (1997). *Democratic Experiments in Africa, Regime Transitions in Comparative Perspective,* Cambridge.
25. Interview with a retired military officer who requested for anonymity to discuss the matter freely.
26. See Fred Guweddeko's account of Kabamba attack as published in *Daily Monitor,* issue of February 7, 2016. Available online: http://www.monitor.co.ug/SpecialReports/NRA-attack-on-Kabamba-causes-tension-between-rebel-groups/-/688342/3065428/-/item/1/-/a8p4n5z/-/index.html.
27. Interview with Dr. Sabiti Makara, Political Historian and Senior Lecturer at Makerere University, Kampala, Uganda (May 23, 2015).
28. Ondoga A. (1998) *Museveni's Long March: From FRELIMO to the National Resistance Movement*. London: Pluto Press.
29. Ondoga A (1998) ibid.
30. Mwakikagile G. (2012) *Obote to Museveni: Political Transformation in Uganda since Independence*. New Africa Press. pp. 215–216.
31. Mutibwa P. (1992) *Uganda since Independence: A Story of Unfulfilled Hopes*. Africa World Press, London.
32. Acopy of the peace agreement is available online one UN website: peacemaker.un.org/sites/peacemaker.un.org/files/UG_851217_The%20Uganda%20Peace%20Talks%20Agreement.pdf.
33. Interview with Maj. Barigye Bahoko, the deputy Chief Political Commissar of Ugandan Military Kampala, Uganda (July 17, 2016).

34. The Observer (2015) "UPDF through the years; is it professional now?" 5 February. Available online http://www.observer.ug/news-headlines/23573-updf-through-the-years-is-it-professional-now.
35. Interview with colonel Barigye Bahoko ibid.
36. Interview with Col. Shaban Bantariza, (NALI), government Deputy Spokesperson, April 25, 2017.
37. Pearce J. (2015) *Political Identity and Conflict in Central Angola, 1975–2002.* African Studies, Cambridge University Press, Cambridge.
38. Clapham C. (1998) "Introduction: analyzing African insurgencies" in: Clapham, Christopher. *African Guerrillas*. pp. 1–18. Also see, Compagnon, Daniel (1998) "Somali armed movements" in: Clapham, Christopher, *African Guerrillas*, 7. 3–90.
39. Douglas J. (2003). *The Root Causes of Sudan's Civil Wars.* Oxford: James Currey.
40. Kriger N. (1992) *Zimbabwe's Guerrilla War: peasant voices.* Cambridge University Press. pp. 152–7, 238.
41. Interview with Maj. John Kazoora (a former NRA fighter-turned-Museveni critic) ibid.
42. Interview with Maj. John Kazoora, ibid.
43. Interview with Bernard Sabiti, a Kampala-based governance expert (May 13, 2016).
44. Interview with Bernard Sabiti ibid.
45. Interview with Journalist Charles Odoobo-Bichachi, the Managing Editor of Daily Monitor, Uganda's largest Independent Newspaper (May 20, 2015).
46. Interview with officer (O2) who requested for anonymity in order to discuss the matter freely.
47. Interview with Maj. John Kazoora ibid.
48. Interview with Maj. John Kazoora. Ibid.
49. Kasfir N (2005) "Guerrillas and Civilian Participation: The National Resistance Army in Uganda, 1981–86." *The Journal of Modern African Studies*, vol. 43, no. 2, 2005, pp. 271–296.
50. Interview with Asuman Bisika, regional security analyst (May 17, 2015).
51. Kriger, N. (1988). The Zimbabwean war of liberation: struggles within the struggle. *Journal of Southern African Studies, 14*(2), 304–322.

52. Interview with Col. Felix Kulayigye. ibid.
53. Interview with Felix Kulaigye. ibid.
54. Interview with Felix Kulayigye. ibid.
55. Museveni Y.K. (1971) "Fanon's Theory of Violence: Its Verification in Liberated Mozambique." In N.M. Shamuyarira, editor. *Essays on the Liberation of Southern Africa*. Dar Es Salaam: Tanzanian Publishing House.
56. Museveni, K. Yoweri (1971) p. 20.
57. Col. Felix Kulayigye. Ibid.
58. Schubert F. (2006) "Guerrillas Don't Die Easily": Everyday life in war time and the guerrilla myth in the National Resistance Army in Uganda-1981–1986" International Review of Social History 51 (2006), pp. 93–111.
59. Interview with John Kazoora. Ibid.
60. Interview with Maj. Ba-Hoku Barigye. Ibid.
61. Interview with Col. Felix Kulayigye. ibid.
62. New Vision (2012) "Mogadishu: Museveni responds to Obbo" May 7. Available online at: http://www.newvision.co.ug/new_vision/news/1301448/mogadishu-museveni-responds-obbo.
63. See, for example, State House Statement issued on September 14th, 2016, Entebbe, Uganda. Available online at http://www.statehouse.go.ug/media/news/2016/09/14/%E2%80%9Creject-pseudo-ideology%E2%80%9D-%E2%80%93-president-museveni-tells-updf-soldiers-mogadishu.
64. Interview with Col. Shaban Bantariza. ibid.

CHAPTER 3

From Rebels to Regime Allies: Coercion, Co-optation, and Neutralization of Armed Rivals

When the NRA seized power in 1986, it inherited a fractured state and a society marked by deeply entrenched social divisions. Preceding decade had been marred by extreme violence, culminating in some of the worst human atrocities in the country's post-colonial history. As previously explained, decades of political turmoil and economic mismanagement had already crippled the economy, but Idi Amin's decision in 1972 to expel approximately 40,000 Ugandans of Asian descent further accelerated economic collapse.[1] Aiming to indigenize the economy, Amin confiscated Asians homes, businesses, and factories and redistributed them to regime loyalists under the guise of creating a new class of "black millionaires".[2] He justified the expulsion by arguing that Asians monopolized Uganda's economic life and that national wealth should rest in the hands of citizens.[3] However, the Asians had long served as the backbone of commerce and industry, and Amin's cronies who replaced Asian businessmen lacked the expertise to manage the confiscated enterprises. By the time the NRA assumed power, Uganda's economy was in tatters. The national treasury was depleted, per capita incomes had plummeted, investment had evaporated, and consumer goods were scarce. A breakdown in food production and supply chains led to widespread shortages and the emergence of *magendo*, or black-market trade, as an alternative means of survival.[4]

G. Bareebe, *Social Structures and the Making of Museveni's Civil-Authoritarian Regime in Uganda*,
https://doi.org/10.1007/978-3-032-14015-9_3

Exacerbating the situation was the NRA's violent seizure of power in 1986, which provoked a new wave of insurgencies—many bearing distinct ethnic and regional identities. These included, among others, the Holy Spirit Movement (HSM), the National Army for the Liberation of Uganda (NALU), the West Nile Bank Front (WNBF), the Allied Democratic Forces (ADF), the Lord's Resistance Army (LRA), and the Uganda National Rescue Front (UNRF). The legitimacy of the new NRA administration fundamentally depended on its ability to restore political order, monopolies legitimate violence, revive a collapsed economy, and assert control over a deeply fragmented society marked by entrenched ethnopolitical tensions and regional cleavages. Although the NRA inherited a residual social structure from previous regimes, it had to confront a fundamental Weberian challenge—i.e., asserting its claim to the monopoly of the legitimate use of force in a landscape of continued armed contestation. Thus, the post-conflict terrain was defined by struggles between the NRA and rival armed groups over the control of coercive force—a contestation that sparked recurring political crises and drastically complicated the NRA's efforts to stabilize and consolidate its rule.

In addition to confronting armed insurgencies, the NRA had to navigate a complex web of entrenched social groups that constituted a residual social structure—groups with deeply entrenched interests shaped by Uganda's turbulent history.[5] These included the Catholic and Protestant Churches, various monarchies, landed elites, and a stratified political class. Uganda's long-standing patterns of socio-economic and political exclusion had recurringly sparked violent insurrections.[6] The NRA leadership understood that relying solely on repression and exclusionary governance would likely reignite instability.[7] In response, President Museveni and his inner circle developed a hybrid strategy that combined coercion with co-optation, alliance-building, and eventually, the decentralization of power. This approach was aimed at responding to entrenched power structures while minimizing the risks of renewed conflict. These seemingly contradictory strategies manifested in two significant ways. First, the NRA employed coercive force to pacify the country, operating on the belief that establishing a decisive monopoly over violence was essential to deterring rebellion. Unlike previous regimes that struggled to contain insurgencies, the NRA moved swiftly and forcefully to crush armed groups that challenged its authority—signaling that armed resistance would not be tolerated. Second, the NRA recognized that overreliance on repression could turn counterproductive. Given Uganda's history of resistance to authoritarian rule, excessive coercion risked alienating civilians and radicalizing previously moderate actors.[8] As such, even while deploying force, the NRA actively co-opted its adversaries, integrated remnants of former armies into its ranks and forged pragmatic alliances to broaden its political base.

Co-optation of Armed Adversaries

Co-optation is a widely used concept in political science to describe the formal and informal mechanisms through which strategic actors—whether inside or outside the ruling elite—are integrated into the governing coalition.[9] Authoritarian regimes that engage in strategic co-optation aim to broaden their support base, defuse opposition, and legitimize their authority without relying exclusively on coercion. As Christian von Haldenwang[10] argues, co-optation serves to reduce regime stress and contain potential challengers before they escalate into existential threats. It functions as a preventive and adaptive strategy in contexts of elite fragmentation or societal unrest. Similarly, Gandhi and Przeworski[11] identify co-optation as a cornerstone of authoritarian durability, noting how regime use it to distribute rents and incorporate rivals. Other scholars underscore the legitimation role of co-optation in authoritarian contexts. André Bank, in his study of Arab regimes, highlights how co-optation is instrumentalized to manufacture regime consent, particularly in hybrid and neopatrimonial systems.[12] Helga Baumgarten situates co-optation within broader strategies of authoritarian consolidation, in which regimes combine ideological appeals, material patronage, and selective inclusion to stabilize rule.[13] This aligns with Gerschewski's triadic model of authoritarian resilience, where co-optation is one of three pillars—alongside repression and legitimation—that regimes balance dynamically depending on the threat environment.[14]

The NRA's use of co-optation closely reflects both the dynamics identified in major scholarship and important adaptations. Whereas much of the literature emphasizes the integration of political rivals through formal institutions or patronage networks, the NRA operated in a post-conflict environment where the boundaries between military and political actors were fluid, and where many potential rivals commanded their own armed forces. In this setting, co-optation was not limited to elite bargaining in legislative chambers or bureaucratic appointments—it often involved the direct incorporation of former adversaries into the army, other security organs, or the political structures. This militarized form of co-optation allowed the new regime to manage immediate security threats while reconfiguring Uganda's political landscape in ways that entrenched its dominance.

The post-1986 consolidation of the regime was, in large part, a product of the NRA's ability to entwine strategic co-optation with selective—and at times brutal—coercion. Rather than choosing between accommodation and repression, the NRA employed both with notable flexibility and adaptability. Armed rivals, former regime loyalists, disaffected ethnic constituencies, and emerging rebel factions were militarily defeated, bought off, or absorbed into the ruling coalition. This hybrid approach not only neutralized immediate armed threats but also allowed the regime to project the image of an inclusive, national, broad-based government. In practice, co-optation did not displace coercion; it complemented it, producing a grey zone in which consent, fear, and opportunism coexisted and sustained the NRA/NRM's dominance. In what follows, I examine how the NRA blended coercion and co-optation against armed rivals, and how this strategic synthesis proved instrumental to its post-1986 consolidation of power.

The Holy Spirit Movement (HSM)

Shortly after Museveni's NRA came to power, a new rebel group—the Holy Spirit Movement (HSM)—emerged to challenge NRA authority.[15] While accounts of the HSM's origins vary, there is broad consensus that its rise was rooted in the NRA's violent pacification campaigns, especially in northern and eastern Uganda.[16] One version of events holds that following the NRA's ascent, rogue elements within its ranks targeted ex-servicemen from the previous regimes and persecuted communities, particularly those from the north and eastern Uganda, who had supported Obote's government. Beginning in February 1986, NRA units reportedly arrested civilians and suspected UNLA remnants in districts such as Tororo, Lira, Kitgum, and Mbale. High-profile figures like Maj. Odur, then head of the military hospital at Mbuya, were arrested on suspicion of plotting to restore the former regime. However, these actions provoked an immediate and violent backlash. Northern ethnic groups mobilized against NRA through the Uganda People's Democratic Movement/Army (UPDM/A), led by Gen. Bazillio Okello.

The UPDA's military campaign was quickly crushed, most notably when its forces were defeated by the NRA's 35th Battalion under the command of Maj. George William Matovu. Despite the UPDA's collapse, the NRA's repressive operations continued, particularly in Teso, where brutal counterinsurgency campaigns were launched against the Uganda People's Army (UPA), led by Peter Otai, a former minister in Obote's administration.[17] Small armed resistance persisted as the NRA's tactics became increasingly violent and indiscriminate. In January 1987, Fred Rwigyema, then commanding NRA operations in the north, provoked widespread outrage after ordering Acholi elders to assemble young men at Corner Kilak for a supposed meeting.[18] Once gathered, the men were marched into a nearby bush where they were detained without food or water. According to eyewitnesses, gunfire erupted the next morning from all directions, and many detainees were killed on suspicion of being rebel collaborators. When asked by journalists to justify the killings, Rwigyema responded with defiance rather than remorse:

> We killed about 350, and these are the bodies we have counted. There are many more bodies lying in the field. These are the ones we have counted so far. The number of the dead could be more than 600... We were surprised to see the rebels coming at us without taking cover. We kept massacring them, but they kept coming, and we killed so many.[19]

President Museveni later visited the area on January 18, 1987, and likewise defended the mass killing. Speaking to local people, he stated:

> The rebels attacked us at a place called Corner Kilak, 20 miles south of Kitgum. They came in while singing and shouting; our people [NRA soldiers] massacred those chaps. They approached us frontally. This gave us a very good chance because they exposed themselves; so, on Sunday, we surrounded them and massacred them. We massacred them very badly.[20]

Museveni's open justification of the killings stunned observers who had previously praised the discipline and restraint of the NRA guerrilla fighters. In a sharply worded letter, Atwoma Okeny, the head of the Uganda Peace Society, condemned what he called the NRA's "scorched-earth policy," accusing the government of unleashing an unprecedented reign of terror in the north. He wrote:

> Reports of incredible atrocities have been, by and large, corroborated by the government-owned [newspaper] The New Vision of 7th September, 1st and 16th November 1988... Mr. President, the severity and magnitude of the scorched-earth policy has reached proportions which [have] poisoned the minds of the people who are facing the onslaught, that it is the beginning of the implementation of the often publicly uttered statements by high-ranking NRM officials to exterminate a people.[21]

Despite mounting public outcry and criticism from civil society actors, the NRA did not abandon its reliance on force. However, it did begin to adapt its approach—gradually shifting toward a more flexible and differentiated strategy that combined coercion with co-optation, collaboration, and, in some cases, assimilation. The application of these strategies was not uniform; rather, they varied according to the nature, strength, and sociopolitical embeddedness of the opponents the regime faced.

The magnitude of the NRA's brutal counterinsurgency operations—and the impunity with which they were often carried out—contributed to the rise of a new insurgent movement called the Holy Spirit Movement (HSM), led by Alice Auma Lakwena.[22] The HSM had both a political arm (the Holy Spirit Movement) and a military wing (the Holy Spirit Mobile Forces), with Lakwena serving simultaneously as spiritual leader, political figurehead, and military commander.[23] The movement capitalized on deep political and ethnic divisions, drawing support from communities in northern Uganda who were enraged by the NRA's violent pacification campaigns. At the same time, the ethnic composition of the NRA—largely dominated by Bantu groups such as the Banyankole and Baganda—provoked resentment among northern ethnic groups, particularly the Acholi and Langi, who had been closely tied to previous regimes and now felt targeted by the new government.

The HSM's early military offensives caught the NRA by surprise due to their unexpected level of organization and tactical coordination. In November and December 1986, Lakwena's forces launched attacks on NRA positions in Kilak and Pajule, defeating government units and seizing significant quantities of ammunition. These military successes were deeply imbued with spiritual meaning. Lakwena claimed to have received a divine prophecy instructing her to save her people from the tyranny of the NRA. Allegations of looting, rape, and murder by NRA forces—especially by the 35th Battalion in Kitgum—further reinforced her prophetic narrative and enhanced her legitimacy among northern communities.[24]

As former spiritual healer and priest, Lakwena explained her transition to armed rebellion as a response to divine revelation. Continuing her healing practice, she argued, had become futile in the face of the NRA's violence.[25] As she put it: *"It is useless to cure a man today only that he be killed [by the NRA] the next."*[26] According to her, God had instructed her to shift from spiritual healing to political liberation. This fusion of religious salvation and anti-regime resistance proved especially compelling to disillusioned Acholi youth, many of whom joined her cause.[27]

To outside observers, the HSM's blend of Christian fundamentalism, Acholi nationalism, and African mysticism appeared strange, even irrational. But for many within the region, Lakwena's spiritual charisma held real power. Her followers believed she was divinely guided, and her authority remained intact even after battlefield losses. When her forces suffered casualties, she attributed the defeats not to tactical failure but to the spiritual shortcomings of those who had died—arguing they had failed to fully adhere to the demands of the Holy Spirit. Survivors, by contrast, were celebrated for their obedience and were said to have been spiritually protected.[28]

Through this powerful mix of faith, identity, and political grievance, the HSM emerged as a serious threat to the NRA's consolidation of power in the north, complicating the regime's efforts to pacify the region through force alone. The HSM was the earliest and most serious tests to the new NRA leadership in important ways: First, Lakwena was remarkably effective at fusing a message of political liberation with spiritual prophecy, enabling her to mobilize fighters with a deep sense of mission and a fearless resolve. Second, unlike the NRA—which was widely unpopular in northern Uganda—the HSM quickly garnered support from the Acholi and other marginalized northern communities. Third, like the NRA in its early guerrilla phase, the HSM enforced strict discipline among its fighters, including clear codes of conduct regarding the treatment of civilians—further boosting its legitimacy in the eyes of local populations.

The NRA dismissed the HSM's spiritual ideology as irrational and absurd, characterizing it as a product of delusion and mysticism.[29] Rather than treating the HSM as a political actor with legitimate grievances, the NRA chose not to open any channels of dialogue or negotiation. This refusal to engage diplomatically, coupled with the military pressure it exerted, ultimately drove Lakwena into launching increasingly desperate offensives. In 1987, the HSM attempted an ambitious military advance to capture Lira town as a strategic springboard toward the capital, Kampala.

The group also massed fighters near Jinja, operating in the Kakira sugar plantations just 90 kilometers from the capital. In response, the NRA launched a fierce and decisive counteroffensive, crushing the HSM forces at Kakira.[30] The defeat was devastating as hundreds of fighters were killed or captured, and the movement was effectively destroyed. Lakwena fled into exile in Kenya, where she lived in a refugee camp until her death in 2007.

Several lessons emerge from this early engagement that would go on to shape the NRA's broader strategy for dealing with armed rivals. First, the NRA did not regard the HSM as a legitimate political actor but rather as a destabilizing force that needed to be swiftly eliminated. Its strategy emphasized rapid and overwhelming military suppression, culminating in the HSM's decisive defeat at Kakira. This victory reinforced the NRA's belief that early and uncompromising use of force could serve as a powerful deterrent to future insurgents.

Second, the NRA paired its military campaign with a discursive strategy aimed at delegitimizing the HSM. By portraying Lakwena's spiritual ideology as irrational and immersed in superstition, the regime sought to erode the movement's moral and intellectual credibility, both domestically and internationally. This framing allowed the NRA to justify its military actions and dismiss the group's grievances as illegitimate.

Third, the NRA refused to engage in any form of negotiations with the HSM, despite multiple calls for dialogue. Unlike later rebel groups such as the LRA, FUNA, UNRF, and WNBF—where peace talks were eventually entertained—the HSM was deemed unworthy of political engagement. This set a precedent within the NRA's strategic thinking: not all challengers deserved negotiation, particularly those lacking a clear political platform or operating outside conventional ideological frameworks.

Finally, while the NRA achieved a decisive military victory over the HSM, it proved to be a short-term tactical success rather than a long-term solution. The deeper structural issues that had given rise to the HSM—particularly ethno-regional marginalization, political exclusion, and ongoing human rights abuses—remained unaddressed. In failing to confront these root causes, the NRA inadvertently paved the way for more enduring and complex insurgencies, most notably the Lord's Resistance Army (LRA). To the NRA, the lesson was clear: military defeat of one rebel group does not eliminate the broader conditions that generate armed resistance.

Aware of the deep-rooted grievances among northern ethnic groups that had fueled insurgency against the NRA, President Museveni extended an olive branch to former HSM leaders through a dialogue convened by the Acholi Cultural Leaders' Forum. In these talks, he pledged amnesty to HSM leaders exiled in Kenya, marking a calculated shift from confrontation to reconciliation. The government paired this gesture with resettlement packages, including financial assistance and support for income-generating activities to facilitate the return and reintegration of former combatants into their communities. Beyond stabilizing northern Uganda in the post-conflict period, this initiative reflected the NRA's broader strategy of selective co-optation to dismantle residual insurgent networks and cultivate loyalty. By incorporating former adversaries into the web of state patronage, the NRM transformed potential threats into politically manageable allies, extending its authority through a calibrated mix of material inducement and symbolic accommodation.

Co-optation of Insurgent Groups in the West Nile Region

While still grappling with Alice Lakwena's Holy Spirit Movement in northern Uganda, the NRA also faced the rise of three insurgent groups in the West Nile region: the Former Uganda National Army (FUNA), the Uganda National Rescue Front (UNRF I and II), and the West Nile Bank Front (WNBF). These groups were primarily composed of former soldiers from the Amin era who had retreated to West Nile following Amin's overthrow in 1979. Their insurgency was largely driven by the NRA's indiscriminate reprisals against ex-Amin loyalists and their ethnic kin, fueling a determination to resist state persecution and defend their communities.

Although the insurgency remained geographically confined to West Nile, it posed a serious threat to regional stability and tested the NRA's capacity to guarantee post-conflict peace and stability. Initially, these rebel groups enjoyed support from local populations who saw them as defenders of a historically marginalized region. However, this popular backing began to erode as civilians increasingly bore the brunt of the violence. Before long, the NRA leadership recognized that—unlike Lakwena's HSM—these former Amin-era soldiers were highly trained, battle-hardened, and possessed the organizational discipline necessary to mount a sustained and credible military challenge to the new regime.

As a result, the NRA adopted a more pragmatic approach. Museveni publicly pledged to end revenge killings against former Amin soldiers and encouraged them to return home peacefully. While some UNRF members responded positively and began returning from exile, others were arrested upon return, prompting renewed suspicion and the formation of UNRF II. At the same time, the WNBF, led by Juma Oris, exploited this atmosphere of mistrust and regional marginalization to expand its ranks and continue the rebellion.

Unlike the military-first strategy employed against the HSM, the NRA pursued a multi-pronged strategy in West Nile that blended covert negotiations, public amnesties, and community engagement. Within the NRA leadership, there was consensus that that West-Nile based rebel groups presented a more serious and politically complex challenge. First, they possessed military expertise. Second, they drew legitimacy from grievances rooted in regional exclusion and NRA's reprisals. Compounding the threat was a lack of reliable intelligence on the number and location of these fighters. Some NRA officials expressed fears that remnants of Amin's entire army were poised for a comeback. Determined to avoid the mistakes of earlier regimes, the NRA pursued negotiations aimed at integrating former combatants into the new military structure as both a gesture of reconciliation and a strategy for state consolidation. Formal talks between the government and the UNRF began in the late 1980s. These culminated in a peace agreement under which UNRF fighters were granted amnesty, their military ranks recognized, and those unwilling to rejoin the army permitted to retire. UNRF leader Gen. Moses Ali—once a prominent Amin official—was not only reintegrated into the NRA's top structure but also appointed First Deputy Prime Minister and Deputy Leader of Government Business in Parliament.

Building on this success, the government signed a similar peace accord with UNRF II, led by Maj. Gen. Ali Bamuze. The 2002 agreement marked the formal end of the West Nile insurgency. Bamuze and his fighters were fully integrated into the national army, with the government honoring their ranks and offering support for resettlement. Reflecting on the negotiations, Museveni remarked that "the NRM does not keep grudges and is not vindictive."[31] One senior NRA officer affirmed this sentiment, noting:

> They [the former Amin soldiers] had genuine grievances and were open to negotiations. The government listened, and we have now integrated

> them into our national army. In the NRA, we believe that negotiation and consensus-building are part of state-building. We understood that not every conflict can be resolved by force.[32]

Importantly, the successful resolution of the West Nile insurgency was not solely the result of state action. Local elders played a pivotal role in facilitating dialogue and building trust between the government and rebel groups. The Aringa-Obongi Peace Initiative Committee (AROPIC), led by respected local figures, traversed the remote areas of South Sudan to engage rebels and encourage them to disarm. Sheikh Haruna Amin Maga, one of the key mediators, recalled: "We had structures up to the grassroots, and the rebels had trust in us. We acted as guarantors of peace—that the government would not come for them—and that is how they gave up their arms."[33]

Maj. Gen. Bamuze later acknowledged that while his rebellion was born out of anger over injustices suffered by his people, the involvement of elders and the government's olive branch compelled him to abandon the war. He stated that, "I started the rebellion because my people had been hurt, but I decided to abandon the fighting because of pressure from the elders and other stakeholders, and the olive branch extended to me by the government."[34]

The NRA's approach to insurgencies in the West Nile region illustrates a pragmatic shift from uncompromising militarism to strategic co-optation and negotiated settlement. Unlike its brutal crackdown on the HSM, the NRA recognized that the insurgent groups in West Nile—composed of former Amin-era soldiers—posed not only a credible military threat but also represented historically rooted grievances around exclusion, revenge, and regional marginalization. By engaging these groups through a mix of amnesty offers, reintegration programs, and political inclusion, the NRA demonstrated a flexible form of conflict management that prioritizes regime consolidation over violent suppression of armed rivals.

The reintegration of former rebels into the national army, the elevation of figures like Gen. Moses Ali into senior government roles, and the involvement of local elders in peacebuilding all highlight how the NRA deployed co-optation not merely as a tactic of pacification, but as a mechanism for legitimizing its rule in volatile regions. This strategy of inclusion, though selective and ultimately subordinated to regime interests, proved effective in neutralizing armed threats without recourse to war—while also reinforcing the NRM's image as a reconciliatory and non-vindictive. Thus, the lesson from the NRA's West Nile approach is clear: authoritarian durability in post-conflict settings often depends not exclusively on brute force but also the ability to forge bargains with former enemies—and selectively co-opting them into the architecture of the state.

The Lord's Resistance Army (LRA)

As the NRA continued to grapple with the rebellion in West Nile, a new insurgent group emerged in northern Uganda called the Lord's Resistance Army (LRA), led by Joseph Kony.[35] The LRA evolved from remnants of Alice Lakwena's Holy Spirit Movement (HSM), with Kony—a cousin and early follower of Lakwena—assuming leadership after the HSM's collapse. According to various accounts, Kony initially joined Lakwena's spiritual-political movement, serving in her camp as a priest.[36]However, he later claimed to have received his own divine revelation to lead a separate rebellion against the NRA. Lakwena reportedly dismissed Kony's spiritual claims, arguing that he lacked the divine authority to lead. Feeling rejected, Kony parted ways with the HSM.

Following the NRA's defeat of the HSM in 1987, Kony filled the resulting power vacuum by absorbing HSM remnants and incorporating Lakwena's mysticism into his nascent rebel movement. Like Lakwena, Kony portrayed himself as a prophet sent by God to liberate Uganda and establish a new government based on the biblical Ten Commandments. His use of spiritual rhetoric, combined with coercive tactics, instilled fear and loyalty among his followers. Over time, the LRA became known for its extreme brutality, including mass killings and the widespread abduction of children and women for use as soldiers and sex slaves.[37]

Several factors contributed to the LRA's rapid growth and resilience. First, both the HSM and LRA capitalized on widespread resentment in northern Uganda caused by the NRA's indiscriminate counterinsurgency operations and reprisals against communities associated with the previous Obote regime. Second, the LRA exploited long-standing regional disparities and grievances—especially the economic and political marginalization of the north—to recruit fighters and build legitimacy.[38] These structural inequalities, rooted in colonial policies that designated northern Uganda as a labor and military recruitment zone while concentrating economic development in the central and south, were compounded by post-independence regimes and exacerbated under the newly established

NRA rule.[39] For example, under the NRA governance, civil service appointments and military recruitment favored western and southern ethnic groups, further alienating northern communities.[40]Consequently, the LRA gained initial support as a movement resisting both historical and on-going injustices. Unlike the HSM or West Nile insurgent groups, the LRA proved more enduring and capable, sustaining a decades-long protracted armed rebellion against the NRM regime.

The LRA conflict intensified in 1991 when the government launched "Operation North," a counterinsurgency campaign led by then-Defence Minister David Tinyefuza.[41] The operation was marked by widespread human rights abuses, including arbitrary arrests, torture, and extrajudicial killings of Acholi civilians suspected of collaborating with the LRA.[42] These repressive tactics alienated local communities and fueled further support for the insurgency. Government officials blamed the persistence of the LRA on local politicians, cultural figures, and residents who were accused of providing shelter and logistical support to the rebels.[43]

The LRA, employing guerrilla tactics reminiscent of the NRA's own past in Luwero, embedded itself within civilian populations, launching surprise attacks and inflicting significant casualties on government forces.[44] In response, the NRA (later renamed the Uganda People's Defence Forces, UPDF) devised a multi-pronged counterinsurgency strategy comprising: (1) intensified military operations; (2) isolating the LRA from civilian populations; (3) initiating dialogue with moderate LRA factions; and (4) co-opting local elites, particularly those perceived to be sympathetic to the LRA.

A key element of this strategy was the forced displacement of over one million Acholi civilians into internally displaced persons (IDP) camps beginning in 1996.[45] The government justified this move as necessary to separate civilians from rebels, thereby denying the rebels access to food, shelter, and local intelligence.[46] However, this approach created a humanitarian crisis.[47] The IDP camps became epicenters of disease, malnutrition, mortality and famine.[48] By late 1996, reports indicated that more civilians were dying from secondary effects of displacement than from direct violence, with mortality rates reaching an estimated 1,000 deaths per week.[49]

Despite these hardships, civilians did not turn en masse to support the LRA. On the contrary, many began providing intelligence to the UPDF, leading to tactical gains by government soldiers. Kony, who had framed his struggle as a liberation movement for northern Ugandans, grew disillusioned with the corroding support from local Acholi and Langi populations. In retaliation, the LRA escalated its violence against civilians, including mutilations and massacres. Kony infamously justified these atrocities by claiming divine sanction, arguing that those who betrayed the movement deserved death punishment.[50]

With over one million civilians forcibly relocated into internally displaced persons (IDP) camps and the LRA increasingly on the defensive, the Ugandan government initiated the second phase of its counterinsurgency strategy: the co-optation of, and alliance formation with, northern elites. Many of these elites—comprising local politicians, cultural leaders, and religious authorities—had long criticized the government's reluctance to engage Joseph Kony and the LRA in dialogue. A series of consultative meetings were convened between top government officials and representatives of northern Uganda's political, cultural and religious leadership.

Initially, President Museveni and senior military figures were staunchly opposed to any form of negotiation with the LRA. They dismissed Kony as a "madman" lacking any coherent political agenda beyond religious fundamentalism and therefore considered unfit for political engagement.[51] Museveni publicly reiterated his commitment to a military solution, stating, "We shall hunt these terrorists and finish them completely."[52] Similarly, senior figures like General Kahinda Otafiire argued that peace talks would be counterproductive, warning that they might facilitate the consolidation of LRA support within Uganda. He argued that peace talks would pave away for "Kony's people trapped in northern Uganda to join him."[53]

Despite this hardline stance, northern elites persisted in advocating for a negotiated settlement. Many blamed the intransigence of the central government—particularly Museveni's militaristic posture—for prolonging the conflict.[54] Amid these tensions, religious leaders from across the Acholi sub-region formed the Acholi Religious Leaders Peace Initiative (ARLPI) to promote non-violent solutions and to pressure the state to open communication channels with the LRA. The ARLPI brought together influential clerics such as Archbishop John Baptist Odama (Catholic), Bishop Macleod Baker Ochola II (Anglican), and Episcopal Vicar Matthew Ojara, alongside priests like Fr. Carlos Lodulgo and Fr. Joseph Genna. By 1998, the ARLPI was spearheading public events such as *Bedo Piny Pi Kuc* ("sitting down for peace"), which convened formerly abducted children, traditional leaders, and local officials to explore pathways to dialogue and reconciliation.[55]

A central figure in these early negotiations was Betty Bigombe, a prominent Acholi politician and then-Minister for Northern Pacification. Bigombe's efforts symbolized both elite commitment to peace and the role of regional intermediaries in mediating national conflict. Her initial contact with the LRA came via Yusuf Adeke, the head of the Gulu Butchers' Association and a covert sympathizer of the LRA, who facilitated access to rebel commanders. Although initial plans involved joint meetings with religious leaders, they withdrew at the last minute, leaving Bigombe to proceed alone. Reflecting on her decision to engage directly with the LRA, Bigombe later remarked that she had pressed on because she wanted to "persuade Acholi sons and daughters to lay down their weapons."[56]

Despite her determination, Bigombe's efforts were ultimately undermined. Powerful figures within the army and government, some of whom reportedly benefited financially from the ongoing conflict, actively sabotaged the talks.[57] According to Bigombe, while some officials such as Col. Wasswa supported the negotiations, others—most notably Brig. Joram Mugume (NRA Chief of Combat Operations) and Lt. Col. Fred Toolit (Director of Military Intelligence)—resisted. These factions insisted on continuing military operations during the negotiations, thereby eroding the credibility of the process. Eventually, the government issued an ultimatum demanding the rebels surrender or face full-scale attack, effectively collapsing the peace effort. Critics argued that the military believed the government had "caved in too much" to rebel demands.[58]

Nevertheless, some Acholi religious leaders pursued independent contacts with Kony through intermediaries in Kenya. A breakthrough occurred in 1999 when Yusuf Adeke delivered a message from Kony to Anglican Bishop Nelson Onono-Onweng, prompting a covert meeting with LRA commanders and the establishment of informal communication channels. These exchanges contributed to the drafting of Uganda's 1999 Amnesty Law. A second opportunity emerged when Vincent Otti, Kony's deputy, called Archbishop Odama requesting mediation by religious leaders.[59] This prompted renewed engagement by ARLPI figures and traditional leaders, who again took the risk of entering rebel-held areas without government authorization. Their efforts culminated in the Juba Peace Talks, facilitated by a delegation of 28 northern leaders—politicians from both the ruling party and opposition, cultural figures, and religious representatives—who met Kony at his Nabanga hideout along the Sudan-Congo border. This delegation, led by then Gulu District Chairman Norbert Mao, signaled the growing unity among Acholi elites in pursuit of a negotiated settlement.

Initially skeptical of these leaders' involvement, the government came to recognize the strategic value of co-opting them. Museveni personally met with prominent Acholi elites—including Odama and Ochola—to build support for state-led pacification efforts. The endorsement of local elites gradually shifted public opinion in the north against the LRA, in part because of widespread exhaustion from violence and displacement.[60] The state's shift from brute force to a more inclusive strategy helped undermine the LRA's support base. For instance, when the government encouraged civilians to form self-defense groups armed with bows and arrows, local elites who had previously opposed military operations did not oppose the initiative, leading to a surprising high level of community participation.

Beyond co-opting elites, the government also targeted LRA commanders for defection. Offers of reintegration into the national army with retention of rank and promise of promotion persuaded several senior commanders—including Caesar Acellam, Obur Nyeko Okuti, and Alex Opoka—to defect and subsequently aid government forces. Though the inclusion of underage abductees in these programs sparked criticism, government officials defended the practice as a lesser evil, arguing that it prevented return to the bush and allowed for reintegration. This strategy of co-optation proved highly effective in rebranding the government as conciliatory and non-vindictive. Former rebels were often surprised by their reception and cited respectful treatment as evidence of a genuine reconciliation effort. One former LRA commander remarked, "I surrendered because I want to be the sacrifice of peace… if I am killed, let it be for peace."[61] Many were shocked to find they were not only spared but absorbed into the army.

The above discussion reveals the NRM's hybrid strategy of combining coercion with co-optation and integration—a marked contrast to similar post-conflict regimes such as Rwanda's Rwanda's RPF, which primarily consolidated power through purges and exclusion of rivals. While the NRM actively sought to co-opt former armed adversaries and incorporate them into state institutions, the RPF pursued a more zero-sum approach that marginalized or eliminated potential competitors to secure tight control. This divergence reflects differing political calculations and contexts. Uganda's complex ethnic dynamics and the protracted nature of its insurgency made inclusion a pragmatic necessity to avoid reigniting conflict among diverse groups. Former rebel commanders from a variety of ethnic groups—including the LRA, UNRF, ADF, and WNBF—were not only co-opted but elevated to senior military positions. By 2005, the national army had absorbed former commanders from multiple insurgent groups. Thousands of lower-ranking combatants were also absorbed. Therefore, co-optation was not purely cynical. Given Uganda's volatile ethnic politics and history of coups and contested transitions, this strategy was arguably necessary to stabilize the country. As one observer put it, "Once stability was attained and the NRA regime cemented its grip on power, the emphasis on ethnic representation and inclusive governance became less of a necessity."[62]

It is not surprising that the NRA found success with this model. During its formative years in Luwero, it had absorbed smaller rebel factions into its guerrilla structure, learning early on that alliance-building could be more effective than confrontation. This legacy is evident in the army, whose senior leadership included numerous former rebels such as Gen. Katumba Wamala (formerly UNLA), Brig. Kasirye Gwanga (UFM), Col. John Paul Ssonko (UFM), Col. Walter Ochora (UNRF), Brig. Nakibus Lakara, and Brig. Paul Lokech—who later led Uganda's AMISOM contingent in Somalia. These examples underscore the long-term institutional impact of the NRA's strategy of co-optation of armed rivals.

The engagement with the LRA revealed the inherent limitations of coercive counterinsurgency and underscored the critical role of Uganda's "residual" social structures—namely, cultural, religious, and political elites—in shaping post-conflict governance. These actors, deeply embedded within the moral and communal fabric of northern Uganda, became key interlocutors at a time when military solutions had failed to deliver sustainable peace. Their sustained efforts not only opened channels for dialogue but also helped redefine the boundaries of legitimate authority in a society fractured by decades of conflict and marginalization. For example, it was under consistent pressure from Acholi political representatives, Catholic and Anglican clergy, and traditional leaders—particularly through institutions like the Acholi Religious Leaders Peace Initiative (ARLPI) and the Ker Kwaro Acholi—that President Museveni reluctantly agreed to explore peace negotiations. These actors did not merely advocate for dialogue from the sidelines; they were instrumental in shaping the substance, structure, and sequencing of the negotiation process. Their influence helped lend credibility to the peace effort and challenged the state's monopolistic claims to authority and conflict resolution.

Therefore, the NRA's co-optation strategy was not purely about national reconciliation. Rather, it was a pragmatic instrument of statecraft, designed to neutralize threats while building a loyal, ethnically calibrated security apparatus. Although former rebels were given positions in the military and sometimes elevated in rank, ultimate control over the security sector remained concentrated in Museveni's inner circle, dominated by individuals from his home region and ethnicity. Thus, while the strategy helped pacify the country and gave the appearance of inclusivity, it ultimately reproduced a personalized, militarized, and ethnically skewed system of rule.

Notes

1. Twaddle, M. (1990) "East African Asians through a Hundred Years" in Clarke, C., Peach, C. and Vertovec, S., eds. *South Asians: Overseas Migration and Ethnicity,* Cambridge, Cambridge University Press.
2. President Idi Amin's Statement on the expulsion of Asians from Uganda. August 9, 1972.
3. Melady T. and Melady M. *Idi Amin Dada: Hitler in Africa* (Kansas: Sheed Andrews and McMeel, 1977), 182.
4. Hansen, H. and Twaddle, M. eds. (1988) *Uganda Now Between Decay and Development* London, James Curry.
5. Green.D. E (2008) "Decentralisation and conflict in Uganda" *Conflict, Security & Development,* 8:4, 427–450.
6. Interview with journalist, Charles Bichachi, Managing editor, Daily Monitor (July 4, 2016).
7. Interview with Dr. Livingstone Ssewangyana, Director Uganda Human Rights Initiative (UHRI).
8. Lindemann, S. 'Just another change of guard? Broad-based politics and civil war in Museveni's Uganda', African Affairs 110, 440 (2011), pp. 387–416.
9. Gandhi & Przeworski (2007), *Authoritarian Institutions and the Survival of Autocrats.*

10. Haldenwang, C. 2017. “The Relevance of Legitimation: A New Framework for Analysis.” *Contemporary Politics* 23(3): 269–86.
11. Gandhi & Przeworski (2007). ibid.
12. Bank, A. (2004) “Rents, Cooptation, and Economized Discourse: Three Dimensions of Political Rule in Jordan, Morocco and Syria.” *Journal of Mediterranean Studies* 14 (1/2), 155–180.
13. Haldenwang, C. (2010) Ibid.
14. Gerschewski, J. (2013). “The three pillars of stability: legitimation, repression, and co-optation in autocratic regimes.” Democratization, 20(1), 13–38. https://doi.org/10.1080/13510347.2013.738860
15. Allen T (1991) “Understanding Alice: Uganda’s Holy Spirit Movement in Context” *Journal of the International African Institute*, Cambridge University Press, Vol. 61, No. 3.
16. Heike B. (198). “Is Alice Lakwena a Witch?’, paper for a conference entitled Uganda: structural adjustment and revolutionary change”, held at Roskilde, Denmark, 20–3 September 1989.
17. Heike B. (1999) ibid. p. 210.
18. Monitor (2013) “The bool Rwigema Never Wrote” October 6. Available online: http://mobile.monitor.co.ug/The-book-Rwigyema-never-wrote/-/691260/2019900/-/format/xhtml/-/q1a0vhz/-/index.html.
19. Kalyegira T. (2012) “Insurgency in the northern and eastern regions in 1986” Daily Monitor (December 12) Available online: https://mobile.monitor.co.ug/specialreports/uganda-50/Insurgency-in-the-northern-and-eastern-regions-in-1986/2471388-1642098-format-xhtml-c3duo9z/index.html.
20. Museveni quoted in: Lukwiya O. R. (2006) “The Acholi Religious Leaders’ Peace Initiative in the Battlefield of Northern Uganda An Example of an integral, enculturated and ecumenical Approach to Pastoral Work in a War Situation” *Graduate dissertation, Leopold-Franzens-Universität Innsbruck*. Available online: http://www.comboni.de/literatur/ochola_diplomarbeit.pdf
21. Atwoma Okeny‘s letter to Museveni quoted in the Monitor of December 12, 2012. Available online: http://www.monitor.co.ug/SpecialReports/ugandaat50/Insurgency-in-the-northern-and-eastern-regions-in-1986/-/1370466/1642098/-/format/xhtml/item/01/-/er8ga6z/-/%2523.
22. Allen T. (1991) ibid. pp. 370–399.

23. Hansen H.B. and Twaddle, M. eds (1995). *Religion and Politics in East Africa: The Period Since Independence*. Athens: Ohio University Press.
24. Gersony, R. (1997): "The Anguish of Northern Uganda: Results of a Field-Based Assessment of the Civil Conflicts in Northern Uganda." Kampala, Report submitted to the US Embassy/USAID mission in Kampala.
25. Gingyera-Pinycwa, A. G. G. (1992): *Northern Uganda in National Politics*, Kampala, Fountain Publishers.
26. Amon C. (2014) "Rejecting the Masculinity of War: Was Alice Auma Lakwena of the Holy Spirit Movement the Messiah of the Acholi?" *Journal of Human and Social Science Research* Vol. 4, No. 1 (2014), 01–07.
27. Heike. B. (1999) Ibid.
28. Hackett R.J., (2001) "False Prophets and the African State: Emergent Issues of Religious Freedom and Conflicts in Uganda", The Journal of Alternative Emergent Religions, Vol. 4, No. 2: 185–203.
29. Interview with Hon. Kaps Fungaroo, Member of Parliament and Shadow Minister for Defence (May 18, 2016).
30. Interview with Col. Felix Kulayigye. Ibid.
31. Museveni's statement on Gen. Bamuze's death October 8, 2015.
32. Interview with Shaban Bantariza.Ibid.
33. Daily Monitor (2014) "Rebel peace brokers cry foul" Oct. 15. Available http://mobile.monitor.co.ug/News/News/Rebel-peace-brokers-cry-foul/-/2466686/2486454/-/format/xhtml/-/nnafwaz/-/index.html.
34. IRN News (2002) "Uganda: Government in peace deal with UNRF-II rebels" 19 June http://reliefweb.int/report/uganda/uganda-government-peace-deal-unrf-ii-rebels.
35. Nyeko B. & Lucima O. (2002) "Profiles of the parties to the conflict." in Lucima, Okello (ed.): *Protracted Conflict, Elusive Peace*: Initiatives to end the Violence in Northern Uganda, London, Conciliation Resources in collaboration with Kacoke Madit.
36. Cline, L. C. (2003): "Spirits and the Cross: Religiously Based Violent Movements in Uganda." *Small Wars and Insurgencies* Vol. 14 (2).

37. Branch, A. (2005): "Neither Peace nor Justice: Political Violence and the Peasantry in Northern Uganda, 1986–1998" *African Studies Quarterly*, Vol. 8 (2).
38. Interview with Hon. Muwanga Kivumbi, Member of Parliament and Shadow Minister for Internal Affairs (July 15, 2016).
39. Doom, R. & Vlassenroot, K. (1999) "Kony's Message: a New Koine? The Lord's Resistance Army in Northern Uganda" *African Affairs*, vol. 98 (390).
40. Dolan, C. (2005) "Explaining War and Its Continuation: The Case of Northern Uganda." Ph.D. thesis submitted to the Development Studies Institute at the London School of Economics and Political Science.
41. Interview with Hon. Kaps Fungaroo. ibid.
42. Interview with Journalist John Njoroge, Kampala, Uganda (May 27, 2016).
43. Interview with Journalist John Njoroge, Kampala, Uganda (May 27, 2016).
44. Adam Branch (2005) "Neither Peace nor Justice: Political Violence and the Peasantry in Northern Uganda, 1986–1998", *African Studies Quarterly* 8/2 (2005) pp. 1–31.
45. Adam Branch (2005). Ibid.
46. Interview with Robert Ssempala, Director Uganda Human Rights Network for journalists (June 21, 2016).
47. Interview with Nicholas Opio, Human Rights Activists, Kampala. (July 7, 2016).
48. Interview with Col. Felix Kulayigye. ibid.
49. UN Integrated Regional Information Networks (IRIN) (1996) "Uganda: ICC Issues Arrest Warrants for LRA Leaders." Available online: https://www.irinnews.org/news/2005/10/07/icc-issues-arrest-warrants-lra-leaders
50. The New York Times (2005) "Atrocity Victims in Uganda Choose to Forgive" April 18, Available online http://www.nytimes.com/2005/04/18/world/africa/atrocity-victims-in-uganda-choose-to-forgive.html.
51. Egeland, J. (2004): "A Ugandan Tragedy" *Washington Post*, November 10, 2004.
52. Daily Monitor (22 September 2006) "No More Talks After Juba Says Museveni" Available at http://allafrica.com/stories/200609220237.html.

53. See the text of his Sydney Peace Prize Lecture, titled: "Saving Our Children from the Scourge of War," Daily Monitor (Kampala), January 8–9, 2006; available at www.essex.ac.uk/armedcon/story_id/000290.html.
54. This is a generally held opinion by many public figures in the north I interacted with, including Hon. Kaps Fungaroo, Hon. Nobert Mao, Hon. Reagan Okumu and many other.
55. Interview with Nicholas Opio. ibid.
56. The Observer (2011 "The roots of war: Betty Bigombe recalls encounter with Kony" September 7. Available: www.observer.ug/news-headlines/14961-the-roots-of-war-betty-bigombe-recalls-encounter-with-kony.
57. Interview with Hon. Kaps Fungeroo. Ibid.
58. Kaps Fungaroo. Ibid.
59. Omara-Otunnu, A. (1995). "The Dynamics of Conflict in Uganda." In Oliver Furley, ed., *Conflict in Africa. London*: Frances Pinter.
60. Interview with Hon. Kaps Fungaroo. Ibid.
61. New Vision (2005) "Rebels turned UPDF commanders" September 5. Available online: www.newvision.co.ug/new_vision/news/1117698/rebels-updf-commanders.
62. Interview with Nicholas Opio. Ibid.

CHAPTER 4

Between Coercion and Accommodation: Authoritarian Bargains in Uganda's Political Settlement

Uganda's recurrent political crises were often traced to deeply embedded sectarianism, which permeated its socio-political and economic institutions and obstructed national integration. The social-structural foundations of post-colonial Ugandan society—marked by entrenched class divisions, monarchism, and religious cleavages—profoundly complicated the state formation process, generating persistent social, economic, political, and ethnic rivalries. These enduring structures nurtured competing sources of legitimacy and identity, continually undermining efforts to build a cohesive nation-state.

Under the colonial rule, religion was deeply politicized, and political competition was often organized along religious lines. The British colonial administration favored the Protestant Church, embedding it within the state apparatus and elevating it as the dominant institutional base of the ruling elite.[1] This privileged status bred resentment and political mobilization among marginalized religious communities, particularly the Catholic church, who saw themselves as excluded from power.[2] These religious cleavages were reflected in post-independence electoral politics. For example, the Democratic Party (DP), primarily Catholic, challenged the Protestant-aligned Uganda People's Congress (UPC), led by Milton Obote. The rivalry between these parties reflected broader struggles between preservation of the status quo and demands for redistribution

G. Bareebe, *Social Structures and the Making of Museveni's Civil-Authoritarian Regime in Uganda*,
https://doi.org/10.1007/978-3-032-14015-9_4

of power—economic, political and symbolic. Sectarian alignments were critical in shaping the contested 1980 elections, which catalyzed the formation of Yoweri Museveni's NRA.[3] Museveni, who ran under the UPM banner, was disillusioned by what he perceived as an entrenched sectarian order dominated by a Protestant-Catholic elites. His subsequent recourse to armed struggle was framed as a radical attempt to dismantle and reconstitute Uganda's exclusionary socio-political structure.[4]

Uganda's sectarian and ethno-regional cleavages more starkly reflected in the composition and politics of the military.[5] Under both colonial and early post-colonial administrations, the armed forces were dominated by Nilotic groups from the north—particularly the Acholi and Langi—whom British colonial authorities had classified as a "martial race" and thus disproportionately recruited into the army.[6] This northern military domination, closely tied to Protestant elites, became a pillar of Obote's first regime. However, the 1971 coup led by Idi Amin—a Muslim from the West Nile region—marked a dramatic shift in the military's ethno-religious balance. Amin's ascent to power marginalized the Acholi-Langi bloc and elevated West Nilers, Muslims, and segments of the Catholic population.

For many Muslims, whose political influence had been sharply curtailed following the rise of Christian missions in the nineteenth century, Amin's presidency symbolized a reclamation of historical status. He did not merely sideline Protestant elites; he actively reconfigured the ideological foundations of the state. Amin declared Islam Uganda's national religion and sought to position the country as an Islamic state, forging close alliances with Muslim-majority countries such as Saudi Arabia and Libya. Uganda's formal admission into the Organization of Islamic Conference (OIC) in 1974 underscored this reorientation.[7] To strengthen his regional and international standing, Amin actively courted prominent Muslim leaders, including Saudi Arabia's King Faisal and Libya's Muammar Gaddafi, both of whom he hosted in Uganda as symbolic gestures of solidarity. By aligning himself with influential Islamic states, Amin projected Uganda as a key player in the Islamic world and reinforced his image as a champion of Islamic causes in sub-Saharan Africa. Amin's religious diplomacy and domestic policies thus entrenched a new axis of power within the state—one that fused religion, ethnicity, and militarism in ways that would have lasting implications for Uganda's governance.

Uganda's enduring challenges in political structuring stem from a combination of its colonial legacy and the unfinished project of state formation, which left fundamental questions of sovereignty, governance, and identity unresolved at independence. In an attempt to manage socio-political pressures—such as class tensions, ethnic divide and localized agitation—British colonial administrators granted special sovereign status to certain kingdoms, most notably Buganda, during the early stages of state consolidation.[8] At independence, four traditional kingdoms were granted semi-federal status, with Buganda enjoying full federal status within what was nominally a republic.[9] This constitutional ambiguity created enduring uncertainty over whether Uganda was to function as a monarchy, a republic, a federation, or a unitary state—an uncertainty that would continue to haunt successive post-independence regimes.

The Buganda Kingdom, for instance, possessed self-governing institutions with many attributes of statehood—complete with its own administrative apparatus, legal systems, and ethno-political leadership, which became a source of persistent friction with the central government.[10] As a monarchy, Buganda enjoyed the privileges and trappings of a state, complete with its own administrative institutions, legal systems, and centralized leadership. In effect, it functioned as a "state within a state"—a status that challenged the authority of the central government and provoked resentment from other kingdoms, such as Bunyoro, that aspired to similar recognition.[11] This arrangement entrenched rival centers of power within Uganda's political order, deepening constitutional ambiguity and laying the foundation for recurring tensions, disputes over authority, and cycles of regime instability. Over time, these unresolved tensions created a structural fault line in Uganda's politics that persisted well beyond independence.

These tensions were exacerbated by the 1900 Buganda Agreement, which fundamentally reshaped Uganda's land tenure system.[12] The agreement granted freehold land rights to the Kabaka and his chiefs, allowing them to acquire land titles over vast tracts of territory. Nearly half of Buganda's land—the most populous and politically influential kingdom—was allocated to the monarchy and its aristocracy, while the rest was claimed by the British crown, leaving the peasantry largely dispossessed. This colonial-era land deal remains one of the most contentious political legacies in Uganda, fueling disputes between the central government and traditional institutions across successive regimes, from Obote and Amin to Lule and Museveni.

The problem extended beyond Buganda. Other traditional kingdoms—though smaller—had existed as semi-autonomous entities before colonial rule and were reluctant to surrender that autonomy to either the colonial administration or the post-independence state. This unresolved "monarchy question" continued to destabilize Ugandan politics. Tensions reached a breaking point during the 1966 Kabaka Crisis, when a constitutional standoff between Buganda and the central government turned violent. Obote ordered a military assault on the Kabaka's palace, resulting in a seven-hour battle that ended with the Kabaka fleeing into exile.[13] In 1967, Obote abolished all kingdoms, a move that effectively eliminated the political base of monarchist elites. However, this decision proved politically disastrous as it alienated a significant segment of the population and deepened regional and cultural resentments. In the years that followed, many monarchists—feeling betrayed and marginalized—would align with Museveni, who promised to restore their kingdoms as part of his broader strategy to topple the Obote regime.[14]

Post-1986 State Formation in Uganda

When the NRA insurgent captured power in 1986, one of the immediate challenges of post-conflict state reconstruction centered on the fundamental question of what kind of state and political order Uganda should adopt. By 1988, internal tensions had begun to surface within the NRA's ranks, particularly around the issue of restoring traditional monarchies. A monarchist faction—especially aligned with Buganda—began pressuring President Museveni to fulfill what they claimed was a wartime promise to reinstate kingdoms in exchange for their support during the guerrilla war. Intellectuals, businessmen, and politicians from Buganda, many of whom had allied with the NRA for this very reason, became increasingly assertive in demanding the restoration of the Buganda monarchy.

This monarchist bloc encountered firm resistance from republican-leaning officers within the NRA leadership. These opponents dismissed the idea of restoring monarchies on ideological grounds, insisting that leadership in a modern republic should not be based on "accidents of birth."[15] Despite their resistance, the debate persisted. Prominent Baganda NRA members such as Abdul Nadduli—who would later serve as a minister in Museveni's cabinet—publicly affirmed that Museveni had indeed promised to restore the kingdom. According to Nadduli, this pledge had played a decisive role in mobilizing Baganda to support the

NRA armed struggle against Obote, who had abolished the kingdoms in 1967.

As tensions mounted, Museveni convened a retreat of the NRA High Command in Gulu to address the impasse. There, he persuaded the leadership that restoring monarchies—in regions where populations strongly supported them—was politically convenient and necessary for national cohesion.[16] Yet still the decision remained deeply divisive. Senior figures like Gen. Kahinda Otafiire openly opposed the move, warning that in a fragile, multi-ethnic state like Uganda, resurrecting autonomous cultural institutions could provoke dangerous centrifugal forces.[17] Some NRA elites also feared that the symbolic power and privileged status of the kings would undermine their own authority within the evolving political order. In a later reflection on this very matter, Museveni acknowledged the controversy surrounding the decision but insisted that restoring the kingdoms was necessary to accommodate communities with deep-rooted cultural attachments.

This episode revealed that Uganda's post-war statecraft was shaped not solely by ideological convictions or coercive actions, but also by the persistent influence of residual social structures—particularly monarchy and religion—and the strategic actions of the NRA elites. The restoration of kingdoms, therefore, was not merely a symbolic cultural concession. It represented a pragmatic compromise, negotiated within a fragmented landscape of post-conflict legitimacy, elite bargaining, and the imperative of national cohesion.

In addition to accommodating monarchist demands, the NRA had to contend with the interests of both the Catholic and Protestant Churches in the formation of the new government. These concessions were not made out of ideological affinity but were strategic accommodations to appease the entrenched ethno-political and religious cleavages that had shaped Uganda's politics since independence. In essence, despite its military triumph, the NRA could not afford to govern with a 'winner-takes-all' approach. It had inherited a convoluted residual social structure—engineered during colonial rule to privilege certain groups over others—and was now compelled to govern within its constraints. In reconstructing the post-civil war regime, the NRA had to navigate a political terrain marked by deeply embedded hierarchies and historically privileged institutions whose status had been elevated under the colonial administration. The legitimacy of the NRA regime, therefore, rested not solely on its monopoly of violence but also on its willingness to engage with powerful actors embedded in the "residual" social structure—traditional monarchies, religious institutions, and ethnic elites—in an effort to construct an inclusive hybrid governance system.

While contemporary literature on state formation emphasizes the transition from personalist rule to depersonalized, institutionalized governance, the NRA's overriding concern was neither the rule of law nor bureaucratic rationalization. Instead, its central project involved accommodating the pre-existing institutional order and assembling a broad-based ruling coalition. This process gave rise to a hybrid civil-authoritarian regime that is neither democratic nor overtly totalitarian. In contrast to similar regimes such as the RPF in Rwanda, where post-genocide governance relied heavily on coercion to suppress dissent, the NRA adopted a strategy of elite co-optation and political assimilation—driven as much by historical cleavages as by internal NRA dynamics. As a result, the emergent hybrid state was deliberately structured to reflect Uganda's multi-ethnic and multi-religious composition. Even within the military—i.e., typically the most exclusive of institutions—the guiding ethos became one of incorporation: the belief that the army "is not an exclusive club" of its original founders but must "absorb its enemies to avoid the enemies of tomorrow."[18]

The NRA clearly recognized that Uganda's prior political systems were structurally unstable—i.e., incapable of accommodating or managing the country's deeply pluralistic character, and thus prone to cycles of crisis and collapse. Learning from the failures of earlier governments that either suppressed or inadequately balanced competing identities, the NRA framed its ascent to power as a "fundamental change" from past regimes. This vision was anchored in the Ten-Point Program, crafted during the guerrilla war, which promised to restructure the state, promote national unity, and address the political, economic, and social fault lines that had long undermined stability.[19] Central to this vision was the commitment to "consolidate national unity and eliminate all forms of sectarianism"[20]—a direct response to the historical fractures that had undermined previous attempts at state-building. The first major step in this reconstruction effort was the decision to outlaw all political parties. Museveni justified this move by arguing that Uganda's previous political instability stemmed largely from sectarian and elite-driven party politics. In his view, political parties—especially those rooted in religion, ethnicity, or region—had perpetuated exclusion and fragmentation rather than national cohesion. As an alternative, the NRA introduced the "Movement System", a no-party framework designed to depoliticize governance and promote inclusive participation without the divisiveness of formal party competition. Under this system, all Ugandans were considered members of the Movement by default, regardless of ideology or background—an approach that Museveni claimed would unite the country and neutralize divisive ethnopolitical identities.

To justify outlawing political parties, Museveni argued that doing so would not end competitive politics, since the "Movement System" would allow individuals to contest for office on personal merit rather than party affiliation, within the umbrella of an all-inclusive political framework. Framing this as a corrective to the divisive, winner-takes-all party politics of the 1960s and 1980s—which, in his view, had exacerbated ethnic cleavages and fueled regime instability, Museveni positioned the Movement as a unifying, non-partisan alternative.

To operationalize this vision, the NRA established a five-tiered governance hierarchy stretching from the village to the district level, intended to embed popular participation while keeping political mobilization under tight central oversight. At the village-level, was Local Council I (LC I), composed of 50–70 households and led by an elected chairperson and a nine-member executive. Above it was LC II, or the parish level, made up of 7–15 villages; its executive comprised LC I chairpersons, and a government-appointed parish chief oversaw service delivery and program implementation—Uganda has around 7,431 parishes. LC III, the sub-county level, typically composed of 6–10 parishes and was managed by a sub-county chief, a technocrat accountable to an elected council functioning like a local parliament; there are about 1,403 sub-counties.[21] LC IV, or the county level, was made up of 5–8 sub-counties and was represented in parliament by a representative elected through adult suffrage. In urban centers, municipalities served as counties with similar representation. At the top was LC V, the district level, composed of 3–5 counties and governed by an elected district council and chairperson; Uganda currently has 135 districts, not including Kampala. This hierarchical system institutionalized governance at the grassroots level and was central to Museveni's project of post-conflict state reconstruction and elite accommodation.

Critics of the NRM regime underscore the danger that Uganda's hierarchical governance structure poses to democratic development.[22] They argue that the system was deliberately engineered to cultivate loyalty to the person of the president and to entrench the dominance of the ruling party.[23] According to Tumwine Patrick, head of advocacy at the Uganda Human Rights Network, Uganda "cannot transition with this kind of structure that is built to enhance a one-party rule." He argues that the system "fuses all government and state institutions with the ruling party," creating a facade that maintains a single individual and party in power under the pretense of multiparty democracy.[24] Drawing on his experience monitoring the 2016 general elections, Tumwine explains that these structures are deeply embedded within the military and NRM control, rendering genuine opposition competition nearly impossible. "One might be misled to think that, at the lower levels of government, individuals have freedom to make decisions," he notes. "The army is in control at every level." He recounts that during the 2016 general elections, soldiers were deployed to their home parishes with explicit instructions and logistical support—including cash and materials such as sugar, tea, soap, and cooking oil—to influence local voters. "These are actions," he concludes, "are designed not to enhance democracy but to keep the existing authority in power."[25]

After cementing its grip at the local governments through a restructured Local Council (LC) system, the NRA turned its attention to consolidating power at the national level. Many Ugandans, weary from years of turmoil and violence, prioritized stability over democratic accountability, and thus paid little attention to the practical implications of the new governance structure. Questions about how the system would integrate Uganda's complex web of socio-political cleavages, or whether a truly broad-based government could be achieved, were largely sidelined. This public apathy—or pragmatic tolerance—gave the NRA a critical breathing space to entrench the "movement system" of government without facing significant opposition or scrutiny.

At the national level, Museveni initiated a power-sharing arrangement that brought together a diverse coalition of actors—including victors from the NRA, individuals from the ousted Obote regime, prominent business elites who had supported the guerrilla war, and figures from traditional political parties.[26] In a gesture of reconciliation and strategic co-optation, Museveni even extended invitations to hardline supporters of Idi Amin to join his administration. As a result, the first decade of Museveni's rule was marked by a carefully curated amalgamation of Uganda's elite: political leaders, monarchists, religious figures, businesspeople, and landed elites. While these individuals represented a wide range of ethno-political and economic constituencies, their inclusion was ultimately controlled by Museveni himself. For example, Paul Ssemogerere, the former president of the Democratic Party (DP), served as internal affairs and later foreign affairs minister; Ruhakana Rugunda, from the Uganda People's Congress (UPC), was appointed health minister; Prof. Edward Kakonge, the first local government minister and architect of Uganda's decentralization, was also drawn from the UPC; and Robert Kitariko, a former DP secretary-general, became the agriculture minister. Other prominent appointees included Ssebaana Kizito (regional affairs, from the DP), Mayanja Nkangi and Samson Kisekka (both staunch monarchists from Buganda), and Andrew Kayiira, a former rebel leader, who was named energy minister. Together, these figures formed Museveni's inaugural Cabinet—the highest executive organ responsible for policymaking and program oversight, with Museveni presiding as Head of State, Head of Government, and Commander-in-Chief.[27]

Beneath the Cabinet was the National Resistance Council (NRC), which had functioned as the NRA's wartime parliament. Initially composed of 38 top NRA commanders selected by virtue of military service, the NRC was exclusive and unelected. However, in April 1987, the NRC was expanded to include all ministers and deputy ministers, growing to over 70 members. Further expansions followed as the regime sought to reflect a more "broad-based" government, though all members continued to be handpicked by Museveni in consultation with the military High Command (HC)—the central authority in the NRA's decision-making apparatus. The HC thus emerged as the nucleus of Uganda's new political order, serving as both the architect and gatekeeper of post-war governance.[28]

The broader question here is: What, precisely, do the actions of the NRA reveal about the nature of post-civil war state reconstruction and regime formation in Uganda? The NRA adopted a distinctive postwar strategy centered not on outright repression but on pragmatic accommodation. It deliberately constructed a political architecture that integrated both loyalists and critics into a broad-based system. This integrative approach served two key purposes: legitimizing NRA rule and neutralizing potential opposition by transforming former rivals into stakeholders with a vested interest in the regime's continuity. It allocated positions of power to adversaries as a way of minimizing resistance and creating an elite coalition bound by mutual interest. During the first decade of NRA rule, this strategy proved highly effective at containing dissent—thanks largely to Museveni's calculated use of co-optation, alliance-building, and concessions. As one senior military officer explained, the objective was to "create a state based on military power but which doesn't use the 'winner-take-all' approach against its rivals."[29] However, this hybrid arrangement also contained the seeds of future instability. By permitting limited internal contestation within the so-called "movement system," the regime projected the veneer of participatory governance while retaining tight control over the state apparatus. Effective power remained militarized and personalized around Museveni himself. In the short term, this fusion of coercive capacity with selective incorporation allowed the NRA to break Uganda's historical cycle of rapid regime collapse by preventing immediate elite fragmentation. However, over the long term, it entrenched a political order in which access to power was mediated through personal patronage and military loyalty rather than institutionalized rules. This perpetuated the structural ambiguity between state and regime that has ensured that political stability remained contingent on the fortunes of the ruling coalition and the authority of the president, rather than on resilient, impersonal institutions.

Containing Monarchies and Contesting Republicanism After 1986

Prior to colonial rule, monarchies in Uganda were constituted as independent, semi-sovereign entities wielding significant political, economic, and cultural authority. The British colonial administration and the subsequent post-independence central governments had to contend with this reality. This tension became most evident in 1966 when President Milton Obote attempted to curtail the political influence of the Buganda Kingdom. The move triggered what became known as the *Kabaka Crisis*, in which Obote ordered a military assault on the Kabaka's palace. The ensuing confrontation lasted seven hours and ultimately forced the Kabaka into exile.[30] A year later, in 1967, Obote abolished all monarchies and declared Uganda a republic. The suppression of Buganda's traditional authority galvanized Baganda's support for Museveni's NRA rebellion, drawn by his promise to restore kingdoms.[31]

The British Colonial administrators initially sought to neutralize monarchical resistance through the incorporation of these institutions into the colonial state apparatus. To mitigate persistent political agitation, the British accorded Ugandan monarchies special sovereign status during the formative years of the protectorate.[32] Four major kingdoms were granted semi-federal status, while Buganda—the most populous and politically assertive—was granted full federal status. This arrangement endured through independence in 1962, preserving multiple centers of authority. As already highlighted, the coexistence of monarchical rule with nascent republican institutions created structural ambiguity about the nature of the Ugandan state. This ambiguity more pronounced in Buganda and was rooted in the 1900 Buganda Agreement, signed between the British and Buganda Kingdom.[33] One of the most consequential outcomes of the agreement was the reconfiguration of land tenure. The Kabakaship and his chiefs were granted large tracts of land under a freehold system, enabling them to register titles and accumulate land. As a result, approximately half of the land in Buganda was allocated to the kingdom and its elites, while the remainder became Crown land. Ordinary peasants were left without legal claims to land ownership. This historical injustice has remained a persistent fault line in Uganda's political landscape, straining relations between Buganda and successive regimes.

After the1986 civil war, one of the most immediate and divisive debates centered on the nature of the new state and the structure of the political regime. Internal fissures emerged within the NRA, particularly over the question of whether to restore Uganda's traditional monarchies. Monarchist elements within the movement—especially those aligned with Buganda—pushed for constitutional recognition of kingdoms, citing prewar promises made by Museveni. These groups argued that the Baganda had overwhelmingly supported the NRA's insurgency precisely because Museveni had pledged to reinstate their monarchy. They were, however, countered by a faction within the NRA that upheld republican ideals. This faction rejected the idea of hereditary rule, asserting that political leadership should not be based on hereditary linage.[34] They feared that legitimizing kingdoms would create competing centers of power that could rival the authority of the central government and undermine the revolutionary egalitarianism the NRA claimed to represent. Despite this opposition, traditional kingdoms were officially reinstated in 1993, but in a redefined form. For instance, they were stripped of political power and reconstituted as cultural institutions—symbolically important but legally subordinated to the republican state.

The triumph of the pro-monarchy faction within the NRA underscores the enduring influence of monarchies as residual social structures in Uganda's post-conflict state formation. Despite their formal abolition in 1967, monarchies—particularly Buganda—remained deeply embedded in Uganda's socio-political fabric. Every post-independence president has had to grapple with this entrenched institution, either by accommodating its demands or attempting to suppress its influence. Conversely, efforts at suppression have often provoked fierce resistance, contributing to regime instability. Both Idi Amin and Milton Obote outlawed monarchies and employed coercive means to neutralize them—strategies that provoked widespread opposition from monarchist constituencies and ultimately contributed to the downfall of their regimes.[35]

Upon taking power in 1986, the NRA sought to break the recurring cycle of tension between the central government and Uganda's traditional monarchies. President Museveni adopted a pragmatic strategy of selective co-optation, symbolic concession, and political collaboration with monarchist institutions. This approach temporarily stabilized relations by incorporating monarchies into a broader framework of cultural accommodation without restoring their political sovereignty. However, the outcomes of this strategy have been mixed. Although officially confined to ceremonial roles, monarchies—particularly Buganda—have remained politically active, often engaging in covert efforts to influence government policy and protect their historical privileges.

The limits of Museveni's co-optation strategy were exposed in September 2009, when Baganda monarchists erupted into violent unrest following a standoff between the state and the Buganda Kingdom. The immediate trigger was the government's decision to prevent the Kabaka of Buganda, Ronald Muwenda Mutebi II, from visiting Bugerere county—a region within Buganda claimed by the Banyara, a minority sub-ethnic group that had declared an autonomous kingdom, allegedly with tacit support from the central government. Many Baganda perceived this to be a deliberate attempt by the Museveni regime to fragment their kingdom and dilute its influence. In response, thousands of Buganda royalists took to the streets in protest, resulting in widespread riots and clashes with security forces.

In additional, Uganda's kingdoms have not only survived formal political marginalization but have also demonstrated a surprising capacity to veto government policies. A notable example occurred in 2005 when the ruling NRM party, leveraging its parliamentary majority, passed the *Regional Tier Bill*. This law proposed the establishment of regional administrations as a compromise to demands for federalism, a system long championed by monarchies as a means of limiting the concentration of power in the presidency. Despite its passage and presidential assent, the law was widely rejected by traditional leaders across the country. Kingdom officials argued that the regional tier model retained excessive central control and failed to meaningfully devolve power. They invoked findings from the 2003 Constitutional Review Commission, which had revealed popular support for a federal system.[36] One Muganda monarchist explained:

> The Regional Tier law still leaves political power in the center... it does not matter how many ministries become controlled by the regional governments; what matters is how much political power the regional governments can exercise. Because of the powers vested in the President, the governance of regional governments can be changed at will—or even suspended.[37]

Despite President Museveni's public promise to implement the regional tier system during the 2010 financial year,[38] the Buganda *Lukiiko* (Kingdom Parliament) formally voted to reject the law. Other kingdoms followed suit by mobilizing grassroots opposition that made implementation politically untenable. The government ultimately shelved the plan, marking a rare and humiliating retreat for President Museveni, who had vowed to enforce the law "by hook or by crook."[39]

A similar outcome emerged with the proposed expansion of Kampala city in 2008. The cabinet approved a bill to create the Greater Kampala Metropolitan Area (GKMA), which would integrate surrounding districts—Wakiso, Mukono, and Mpigi—into a single administrative unit. Buganda Kingdom, which owns much of the land in the targeted areas, vigorously opposed the bill, arguing that the expansion constituted a land grab designed to erode the kingdom's territorial authority. Utilizing its vast media infrastructure—including radio stations, television platforms, and public rallies—the kingdom mounted a successful campaign against the bill. Facing sustained resistance, the cabinet eventually amended the legislation, removing the clause that sought to enlarge city boundaries.[40]

In conclusion, President Museveni is not the first Ugandan leader to see his legislation blocked or rendered unimplementable due to kingdom opposition. In 1975, President Idi Amin issued a land decree that sought to abolish the Mailo land tenure system—a cornerstone of Buganda's traditional authority. Yet monarchist opposition was so intense that the land registry remained effectively intact, and the decree was never fully implemented.[41] These episodes underscore the enduring political salience of Uganda's monarchies. Despite being formally designated as cultural institutions, they retain considerable emotive power to shape, obstruct, or delegitimize government policies—particularly when their economic, territorial or symbolic interests are at stake. This capacity to frustrate central state initiatives reveals a deeper structural feature of Uganda's politics: the persistence of entrenched, semi-autonomous power centers that the central government cannot fully absorb or eliminate.

Accommodating the Interests of Churches

Uganda's post-colonial political development was shaped—and often destabilized—by the deeply entrenched sectarian and religious cleavages embedded in its social structure.[42] Since the colonial era, religion has been a critical axis of political identity and mobilisation.[43] The Catholic-Protestant-Islamic divide not only informed everyday social relations but also structured political competition. Uganda's two main post-independence political parties—the Democratic Party (DP) and the Uganda People's Congress (UPC)—were deeply rooted in these religious fault lines. The DP was largely supported by Catholics, while the Anglican Church and Protestant elites dominated the UPC party.[44] This sectarian polarization played a direct role in shaping political alignments during the disputed 1980 elections. While the Protestant establishment backed UPC's Milton Obote, the Catholic Church threw its weight behind DP's Paul Kawanga Ssemogerere. Although Museveni lost the election running under the Uganda Patriotic Movement (UPM), the perceived manipulation of the process—and its religious undertones—convinced him that Uganda's fractured and exclusionary political order could only be transformed through armed struggle.[45]

The legacy of religious sectarianism posed both a challenge and an opportunity for Museveni after the NRA's military victory in 1986. Cognizant of how religion had historically fueled division and rebellion, Museveni's regime-building strategy deliberately sought to co-opt and neutralize Uganda's powerful religious institutions rather than violently confronting them. His approach to churches mirrored his broader strategy of elite accommodation—i.e., incorporating previously excluded groups—former adversaries, monarchists, ethnic leaders, and religious elites—into a reconstructed political order that offered them recognition, resources, and space for influence, while ultimately centralizing power within the NRM.

This co-optation was facilitated by the shifting role of churches in the post-Amin and post-civil war period. Both the Anglican and Catholic churches, previously seen as complicit in sectarianism and elite rivalry, emerged from the 1979–1986 conflict with renewed legitimacy. Their shared experience of repression under Amin—including the assassination of Archbishop Janani Luwum for speaking out against human rights abuses—had fostered a degree of unity, legitimacy and moral authority.[46] Moreover, their active engagement in post-war recovery—particularly in education, health, and poverty alleviation—enhanced their status as key actors in national reconstruction.

Recognizing this influence, Museveni avoided alienating the churches. Instead, he cultivated cordial relations with both Catholic and Anglican leaders, consulted them on national issues, and frequently invoked shared values of peace and development. This tactical engagement enabled the NRM regime to harness the churches' moral capital while blunting their capacity for organized opposition. By bringing them into the regime's governance structure, Museveni insulated his government from the kind of church-led agitation that had helped delegitimize previous regimes. Therefore, the accommodation of religious institutions was not merely a reflection of Uganda's social realities but a calculated part of Museveni's regime consolidation. It exemplified the NRM's broader post-conflict strategy: forging elite consensus through inclusion and co-optation, defusing sources of resistance, and reconstituting Uganda's fractured society under a centralized but pluralistic regime architecture.

To date, churches remain influential actors in Uganda's political landscape, continuing to shape the country's trajectory on critical issues such as justice, corruption, political pluralism, and human rights. While Museveni's regime has largely succeeded in co-opting religious institutions—often incorporating church leaders into NRM's patronage networks—this co-optation is neither complete nor uncontested. In instances where co-optation falters or regime excesses become too blatant, church leaders have demonstrated a readiness to adopt confrontational strategies, including outspoken public criticism. Prominent clergy regularly condemn state corruption, electoral violence, human rights violations, and social injustice, particularly during election periods or following episodes of state repression. This dynamic was well articulated by a prominent Catholic priest and historian, who emphasized the church's enduring role as a moral counterweight to state power. As he reflected, "The church opposed Idi Amin, opposed Obote's regime, and was determined to ensure that the new NRA regime doesn't oppress the people… When the NRM goes against the church's core principles, the church is not afraid to raise objections."[47] This underscore how religious institutions in Uganda have historically functioned both as partners and as critics of the state, wielding significant normative authority that can either legitimize or challenge ruling regimes.

Public criticism of the NRM by church leaders has been most pronounced during elections and periods of intensified repression.[48] For instance, in 2018, the Archbishop of Kampala, Cyprian Kizito Lwanga, publicly denounced the government for widespread human rights abuses and excessive use of force. In response, President Museveni promptly arranged a personal meeting with the archbishop and held a joint press conference aimed at demonstrating unity and de-escalating tensions between church and state. Further efforts to contain the fallout included inviting senior Catholic leaders, among them the Vatican's envoy to Uganda, for closed-door negotiations—signaling the regime's desire to maintain its symbolic alliance with religious institutions. During the 2021 general elections, Catholic and Anglican leaders condemned the government's violent crackdown on protesters and called for national dialogue to address mounting political grievances. The late Archbishop Lwanga notably demanded an independent audit of the election results, echoing calls from opposition figures. In regions such as Buganda and northern Uganda, where opposition support is robust, local clergy have actively provided moral endorsement to opposition candidates like Kizza Besigye and Robert Kyagulanyi (Bobi Wine), thereby complicating the regime's attempts to consolidate political control. This interplay highlights the churches' dual role as both legitimizers and challengers of the NRM regime, reflecting their embeddedness in Uganda's contested political landscape.

Beyond public criticism, religious leaders in Uganda strategically employ a dual approach that combines outspoken advocacy with discreet lobbying to secure policy concessions from the state. This hybrid engagement underscores their complex position as both moral authorities and influential political actors. The regime has at times co-opted religious elites by incorporating clerics directly into the executive branch. For example, Father Simon Lokodo's tenure as a cabinet minister illustrates how the NRM absorbs religious figures to manage dissent and project inclusivity. Behind closed doors, religious leaders actively engage in negotiations to influence policy decisions and political appointments. In 2016, prominent Catholic clerics acknowledged having advance knowledge of cabinet reshuffles, reflecting direct consultations with President Museveni himself. This pattern highlights the strategic importance Museveni places on maintaining religious representation within government as a tool of political stability. As an Anglican, Museveni has consistently appointed Catholics to key positions—including the vice presidency—in a calculated effort to maintain sectarian balance and mitigate potential discontent from the Catholic majority, thereby reinforcing the regime's broader strategy of managing Uganda's religious and ethnic pluralism through selective inclusion.

In a nutshell, the relationship between the Uganda's religious institutions and the Museveni regime is defined by strategic engagement, moral autonomy, and a delicate balance of cooperation and critique. These institutions have undoubtedly remained ambiguous allies in the NRM's regime-building project. The NRM has managed to co-opt churches into the architecture of post-war governance—through concession, symbolic appointments, and access to state resources. However, they have maintained a dual role--i.e., as partners in regime legitimation and as vigilant guardians of public morality. They remain among the few institutions capable of speaking truth to power, holding the regime to account when its actions violate human rights and democratic norms. This duality makes the church a uniquely potent actor in Uganda's political order—simultaneously inside and outside the regime, both legitimizing and limiting state authority. As such, the church continues to occupy a central but ambivalent position in Museveni's broader regime-building project.

Navigating Interests of Landed Elites

Land, as both a material asset and a symbol of ancestral rights is one of the most politically sensitive and potentially destabilizing issues in Uganda. Uganda's 1998 Land Act recognizes four land tenure systems—Customary, Freehold, Leasehold, and Mailo (Ugandan Land Act, 1998). Among these, the Mailo tenure system is the most politically and legally complex. It establishes a form of dual ownership in which formal landowners, who possess legal title, coexist with *Bibanja* holders—bona fide occupants who have lived on and utilized land for at least twelve years prior to the promulgation of the 1995 Constitution.[49] Though Bibanja holders lack legal title, they are constitutionally protected and represent a vast, politically significant constituency. This creates an inherent tension between landlords and occupants. For instance, while the former commands legal ownership and often social prestige, the latter wield substantial electoral influence due to their sheer numbers and historical claims to the land.

Since the late 1990s, the NRM government has made repeated attempts to modernize Uganda's land ownership system by phasing out traditional tenures and centralizing state control over land. These efforts have been framed as necessary for national development and infrastructure expansion, but they have encountered fierce opposition from monarchies, landed elites, and rural populations.

The entrenched resistance to land reform was illuminated in 2017 when the government introduced Constitution Amendment Bill No. 2, which sought to give the central government powers to compulsorily acquire land for public projects before compensating landowners. The bill triggered widespread backlash across Uganda's regions, uniting traditional landowners—monarchies, landlords, and cultural institutions—into a coordinated opposition front. The Buganda Kingdom, whose Mailo land system was directly threatened, led the charge. The Kabaka (King) of Buganda condemned the bill as "a pain that poses an existential threat to the future generation".[50] Kingdom officials convened a series of land sensitization seminars, aimed at mobilizing monarchists, landowners, and Bibanja holders alike in resistance. A prominent Buganda minister declared that:

> we believe in the constitution that vests all the powers in the hands of the people, and these people are saying this amendment is bad. A law that is not fair cannot work. We will come together and fight to see that it [bill] doesn't go through, and in case it goes through, we shall challenge it.[51]

In response, President Museveni launched a national wide campaign to rally support for the amendment. However, even these public engagements met organized resistance, particularly from powerful landlords and kingdom-aligned elites. The president's inability to push the bill through Parliament—despite his dominant party control—reflected a rare political defeat. Members of his own ruling NRM party publicly distanced themselves from the bill, with some calling it "political suicide".[52] Ultimately, the bill was withdrawn in September 2018.[53]

Previously, the government had approached the question of land tenure for *Bibanja* holders—occupants of *Mailo* land—with caution, recognizing both the political volatility of the issue and the electoral importance of these occupants.[54] In an effort to secure their loyalty and alleviate land insecurity, President Museveni issued several executive directives, and Parliament passed laws aimed at protecting Bibanja holders from unlawful evictions. These measures were designed to portray the regime as a defender of popular interests, particularly in rural areas where land ownership is a central concern. However, despite these legal protections, evictions of Bibanja holders by powerful landlords have continued, especially in Buganda and Bunyoro—the two regions where *Mailo* land is most prevalent and deeply politicized. Moreso, the *Mailo* land system, originally introduced by British colonial authorities, was crafted to solidify the political authority of the Kabaka (king) over his subjects by granting Mailo titles to royal allies and chiefs.[55] This colonial arrangement entrenched a landlord–tenant dynamic that persists today and remains a major source of land conflict. As land values have risen—particularly around urban and peri-urban areas—landlords have increasingly sought to assert their property rights, often at the expense of long-standing tenants.

In collusion, land in Uganda is both a vital resource, a symbol of ancestral rights, and a domain for political contestation. Resistance to land reform, including the 2017 constitutional amendment, underscores the limits of the NRM regime's power and the enduring influence of landlords and traditional monarchies intent on preserving the status quo. Despite legal protections, evictions persist, driven by rising land values and historical landlord–tenant dynamics. Land thus remains a site of social contestation and political negotiation, where policy interventions must navigate historical, cultural, and electoral sensitivities to avoid destabilization.

Dealing with the Mercantile Class

The trajectory of Uganda's mercantile class has been shaped by dramatic historical disruptions, notably under the regime of Idi Amin. In 1972, Amin launched what he termed an "economic war," ostensibly aimed at indigenizing the economy and fostering a new generation of "Black millionaires."[56] This campaign entailed widespread nationalization of private enterprises and the expulsion of over 60,000 Asians, who had been central actors in the country's commercial sector. The consequences were severe economic collapse, institutional decay, and a prolonged period of recovery that extended well beyond Amin's fall. In contrast, the Museveni government repositioned Uganda as a pro-market, investor-friendly state. It pursued neoliberal reforms, liberalized the economy, and facilitated the return of expelled business communities, particularly the Asian Ugandan diaspora. Nonetheless, within this ostensibly liberal framework, the domestic mercantile class has emerged as a decisive actor with the capacity to shape state behavior and policy. Their engagement with the regime exemplifies the complex interplay between economic interests and political power in Uganda, where the consolidation of the mercantile elite reflects both the opportunities and constraints of post-conflict state reconstruction and regime survival.

Currently, most landowners in Uganda—particularly those possessing extensive acreage—form a relatively small yet politically and economically influential mercantile class. Despite its limited size compared to neighboring countries such as Kenya and Tanzania, this business elite has steadily consolidated its power and sway over government economic policies throughout the Museveni era. Their influence stems from a combination of historical legacies and contemporary organizational capacity, positioning them as key stakeholders within Uganda's political economy.

Key business associations such as the Kwagalana Group—a social network of the country's top fifty entrepreneurs—and the Kampala City Traders Association (KACITA) have repeatedly mobilized to block or reverse government policies seen as harmful to their commercial interests.[57] In 2013, for instance, the government introduced a Pre-export Verification of Conformity (PVoC) policy, designed to prevent counterfeit goods from entering Uganda.[58] Although framed as a consumer protection and trade quality measure, the policy was strongly opposed by KACITA and Kwagalana. The two groups mobilized city traders into a coordinated three-day strike, during which businesses were closed and economic activity stalled in Kampala's central business district. Under mounting pressure, the government was forced to withdraw the policy.[59] A similar episode occurred in 2012, when the Central Bank raised the Central Bank Rate (CBR) by 23%, triggering a sharp rise in commercial lending rates.[60] Traders with existing loans faced financial distress as repayment burdens soared.[61] In response, KACITA and Kwagalana once again led a protest campaign, organizing traders across Uganda to close their shops in protest. Their capacity to impose economic paralysis in the capital city underscored their bargaining power. Although the government did not immediately reverse the CBR decision, it was compelled to engage in negotiations with business leaders and offer relief mechanisms, including the temporary suspension of some tax collection activities.[62]

A similar standoff unfolded in July 2024 when the government introduced the Electronic Fiscal Receipting and Invoicing Solution (EFRIS).[63] The system requires traders to purchase an Electronic Fiscal Device (EFD) capable of issuing automated invoices, enabling the Uganda Revenue Authority (URA) to automatically charge Value Added Tax (VAT) on each transaction and combat tax evasion. Traders argued that the 18% VAT, applied each time goods are transferred to another trader or business, amounted to double taxation and would undermine their competitiveness in the region—particularly against East African countries with lower VAT rates. In protest, both small- and medium-sized business owners shut their shops.

For several days, the government and URA defended EFRIS as essential for catching tax evaders and those who underreport sales. As the standoff persisted, President Museveni agreed to meet with traders in an effort to convince them to call off the strike. Thousands gathered at Kololo grounds, where a number were allowed to voice their grievances directly to the President. Many observers were struck by the traders' open defiance, with some bluntly telling Museveni that his regime would be permanently tainted by its decision to press ahead with the unpopular policy.[64] In response, Museveni made several concessions, including directing the URA to remove penalties for those who failed to adopt EFRIS, a move that underscored the power of traders as an organized social group capable of influencing state policy.

Unlike traditional social institutions such as monarchs or landed elites—who derive their power from cultural legitimacy or inherited privilege—business elites exert influence through economic leverage and collective organization. Their capacity to disrupt urban economies gives them a powerful veto over state policy, particularly in the areas of taxation, trade regulation, and financial governance. For the NRM regime, managing the mercantile class requires a careful balancing act. On one hand, the state depends on the business community for revenue generation, employment, and economic stability. On the other, it must avoid policies that trigger capital flight, urban unrest, or elite alienation. As a result, the government often accommodates their demands—either by amending controversial policies or through private negotiations. Their ability to resist state policy without resorting to formal political opposition demonstrates that economic elites can exert de facto political influence even in a tightly controlled regime. Making concession to business elites is thus part of the NRM's broader strategy of elite accommodation, which involves selectively empowering influential actors while preserving central political control.

The arguments above highlights the limits of Museveni's co-optation, concession, and alliance-building strategy in the face of deeply entrenched social structures. While the NRM regime has been remarkably effective at neutralizing opposition through patronage and elite inclusion, certain domains—particularly land—remain politically volatile and structurally resistant to centralization. The failure of the 2017 land amendment bill illustrates that even a powerful and long-ruling authoritarian regime cannot easily override historical claims, cultural legitimacy, and entrenched economic interests, especially when those interests align with mass constituencies such as *Bibanja* holders. The land question, therefore, exposes the fragility of regime authority in contexts where elite and popular interests converge.

Navigating this terrain requires the NRM regime to engage in constant political balancing, delicately managing the often-competing demands of landlords, churches, monarchies, and urban business elites. These actors are not simply obstacles to reform—they are structural power centers whose cooperation is essential to political stability, and whose resistance can produce significant policy reversals or political crises. The Museveni's strategy of co-optation and elite accommodation, while not without constraints, has nonetheless enhanced the regime's legitimacy by projecting an image of inclusivity, reducing elite fragmentation, and incorporating key social constituencies into the framework of state power. The durability of Museveni's authoritarian rule in Uganda, therefore, depends not only on the regime's coercive capacity, but also on its ability to manage the enduring power and interests of Uganda's traditional and economic elites.

Notes

1. The correspondence between political parties and religious denominations must be qualified. There are members of different religious denomination in both parties.
2. Mujaju, Akiiki (1976). ibid. p. 5.
3. Jaynes G (1980) "*Counting Votes* Is *Half* the *Fun* as *Obote Wins* in *Uganda*," *New York Times*, 14 December.

4. Gertzel C. (1980) "Uganda after Amin: the continuing search for leadership and control" *African Affairs*, 79: 461–89. Also see, Simon Hardwick (1982) "Administrative aspects of the Uganda elections, December 1980: a comparison with Zimbabwe', Public Administration and Development" 2, 105–12.
5. Ingham K. (1994) *Obote: a Political Biography* London and New York: Routledge, 169–75.
6. Brett, E. A. (1995) "Neutralizing the Use of Force in Uganda: The Rôle of the Military in Politics" *The Journal of Modern African Studies*, 33(1), 129–152.
7. Mittelman J. (1975) *Ideology and Politics in Uganda: From Obote to Amin* Ithaca, NY: Cornell University, 125–30.
8. Kasfir N. (1983) State, *Magendo,* and class formation in Uganda, The Journal of Commonwealth & Comparative Politics, 21:3, 84–103.
9. Interview with Dr. Sabiiti Makara. Ibid.
10. Golooba-Mutebi Fredrick (2011) "Settling the Buganda Question" Indiana University Press, Hutchins Center for African and African American. Transition, No. 106. pp.10–25.
11. Golooba-Mutebi Fredrick (2011) ibid.
12. Golooba-Mutebi Fredrick (2011) ibid.
13. See more information on Buganda Kingdom website available online http://www.buganda.com/crisis66.htm.
14. Interview with Hon. Muwanga Kivumbi. Ibid.
15. Golooba-Mutebi Fredrick (2011). Ibid.
16. Quinn, J. R. (2014), "Tradition?! Traditional Cultural Institutions on Customary Practices in Uganda," Africa *Spectrum*, 49, 3, 29–54.
17. Interview with Bernard Sabiiti ibid.
18. Interview with Col. Felix Kulayigye Ibid.
19. See Museveni's 1986 inauguration speech available at http://observer.ug/component/content/article?id=13388:museveni-1986-2011-from-fundamental-change-to-no-change.
20. See Museveni's1986 Ten-Point Program available online at: http://www.monitor.co.ug/News/National/Musevenis-10Point-Programme-vs-Mbabazis-eight/688334-2753336-dl2d4hz/index.html.

21. Kisakye, J. (1996): "Political background to decentralization", in: Villadsen, Søren; Lubanga, Francis (eds.), *Democratic decentralization in Uganda: A new approach to local governance*, Kampala, Uganda.
22. Interview with Maj. John Kazoora ibid.
23. Interview with Ladislaus Rwakafuzu, a prominent Human Rights lawyer, Kampala, Uganda (June 30, 2017).
24. Interview Tumwine Patrick, the head of advocacy at Uganda Human Rights Network (July 18, 2017).
25. Interview Tumwine Patrick. ibid.
26. Lindemann, S. (2008) "Do inclusive elite bargains matter? A research framework for understanding the causes of civil war in Sub-Saharan Africa", *Crisis States Discussion Papers Series* 15, London: Crisis States Research Centre, London School of Economics.
27. More on this can be found in Articles 98 and 99 of the 1995 Ugandan Constitution.
28. Interview with Dr. Livingston Ssewanyana. ibid.
29. Interview with Col. Felix Kulayigye. ibid.
30. See more information on Buganda Kingdom website available online http://www.buganda.com/crisis66.htm.
31. Interview with Hon. Muwanga Kivumbi. Ibid.
32. Kasfir, 1983 ibid.
33. Golooba-Mutebi Fredrick (2011) ibid.
34. Golooba-Mutebi F., (2011). ibid.
35. Oloka-Onyango, J. (1997) "The Question of Buganda in Contemporary Ugandan Politics." *Journal of Contemporary African Studies* 15.2: 173–89.
36. The Observer, March 27, 2014.
37. A comment from a Buganda kingdom royalist published online by a Pro-Buganda website (ekitibwakyabuganda.com). available online: https://ekitibwakyabuganda.wordpress.com/2009/09/06/why-buganda-refused-the-regional-tier/.
38. The New Vision, October 7, 2009.
39. The New Vision, October 7, 2009.
40. Gina S.L., (2014) "Opposition Politics and Service Delivery in Kampala, Uganda" *Development Policy Review*, 2014, 32 (S1): s39–s60.

41. Kato J., (2007) "Should Mailo Land Tenure be Scrapped" The New Vision (February 25) Available online: https://www.newvision.co.ug/new_vision/news/1170236/mailo-land-tenure-scrapped
42. Carney, J. J. (2017). The politics of ecumenism in Uganda, 1962–1986. *Church History, 86*(3), 765–795.
43. Mujaju B. (1976). ibid.
44. Carney J. (2017). ibid.
45. Gertzel C., (1980) "Uganda after Amin: the continuing search for leadership and control" *African Affairs*, 79: 461-89.
46. Mujaju, B. (1996). Reflections on church and politics in uganda. *The Uganda Journal,43.*
47. Interview with a prominent catholic priest.
48. See for example, AllAfrican.com story of how church leaders in Uganda were openly critical of corruption in Museveni's government. Available online: https://allafrica.com/stories/199906040102.html.
49. GoU Report, 2017.
50. The Observer, August 15, 2017.
51. Statement by Noah Kiyimba, a Buganda Kingdom Cabinet Minister available online http://www.fhri.or.ug/index.php/pages/whats-new/item/204-battle-lines-drawn-as-land-amendment-causes-uproar.
52. The Observer, August 21, 2017.
53. The Parliament of Uganda Website, September 5, 2018.
54. See President Museveni Directive on land evictions available online: https://ugandaradionetwork.com/story/president-stops-all-land-evictions-in-buganda-bunyoro-regions.
55. Elliott D.G., (2005) *Ethnicity and the politics of land tenure reform in central Uganda.* DESTIN Working Paper (05-58). London School of Economics and Political Science. Development Studies Institute, London, UK.
56. Amin's Statement, August 9, 1972.
57. The Monitor October 20, 2019.
58. Bwambale A., (2013) "Assessing traders' strike in Kampala" The Monitor (June 30).
59. Bwambale 2013 ibid.

60. The Central Bank Rate (CBR) is indicative lending rate of the Bank of Uganda (the Central Bank). It is used to fight inflation that once skyrocketed to 30% in 2011.
61. Uganda Radio Network (2012) "Kampala Shops Closed as Traders' Strike Starts" (January 11) https://ugandaradionetwork.com/story/kampala-shops-closed-as-traders-strike-starts.
62. The New Vision, January 12, 2012.
63. URA Statement available https://govinfohub.go.ug/index.php/2024/05/28/ura-commences-waiving-of-efris-penalties/.
64. Daily Monitor (2025) "What became of Museveni's meeting with traders" May 14. https://www.monitor.co.ug/uganda/business/prosper/what-became-of-museveni-s-meeting-with-traders--4619644.

PART II

The Security Architecture and Regime Hegemony Under the NRM Rule

CHAPTER 5

Militarization, Patronage, and State-Building after Civil War

During the 2001 presidential election campaign, Museveni toured the country pledging to professionalize the army—a promise that resonated with both domestic and international audiences concerned about Uganda's history of military coups, mutinies, and political instability. Donors and citizens alike viewed this reformist rhetoric as a potential break from the political turbulence of the past, envisioning a non-partisan, disciplined military as the foundation for democratic consolidation. However, this vision of "professionalization" ultimately proved illusory. Rather than insulating the military from political influence, Museveni subordinated the institutional interests of the Uganda People's Defence Forces (UPDF) to those of the regime, transforming the army into an instrument of regime consolidation rather than a neutral guarantor of democratic stability.

It is therefore unsurprising that, after more than three decades in power, Museveni has consistently resisted both internal and external pressures to depoliticize and de-ethnicize the military. As a result, the Ugandan military has become increasingly controversial within the country's body politic due to its instrumental role in safeguarding regime survival. Museveni's approach makes clear that any reforms toward professionalizing the army will proceed on his terms—incrementally and only insofar as they serve the strategic interests of regime consolidation.

G. Bareebe, *Social Structures and the Making of Museveni's Civil-Authoritarian Regime in Uganda*,
https://doi.org/10.1007/978-3-032-14015-9_5

Between 2002 and 2004, Uganda undertook an ambitious defence review process aimed at professionalizing the army and enhancing military efficiency. In the wake of the review, the UPDF began implementing a series of recommended reforms intended to redefine its role as a conventional force focused on external defence, leaving internal security functions to the police. While these reforms improved the UPDF's technical proficiency, they failed to depoliticize the institution. The army remains a highly personalized entity, with its structure and command culture closely bound to President Museveni. In what follows, I examine the defence review process and its key recommendations, showing how the reforms strengthened the UPDF's operational capacity but ultimately fell short of insulating it from political control.

Reforming the Army, Preserving the Regime

Two decades after capturing power, elites within the NRA began advocating for a shift in the military's ideological orientation and strategic vision. They argued that, despite its military victory, the NRA had fundamentally remained a partisan force with limited appeal beyond its bush war comrades.[1] This problem was compounded by the atrocities committed by the NRA during its pacification campaigns in northern and eastern Uganda, which cast doubt on its stated commitment to democracy and human rights. At the same time, the government continued to allocate a large share of the national budget to military expenditure, much of which was lost through corruption and embezzlement.[2]

By the late 1990s and early 2000s, international donors began linking security to development, emphasizing conflict resolution and the reduction of military forces in fragile states.[3] Security sector reform (SSR) emerged as a key strategy for conflict prevention and good governance. Uganda's lack of military accountability and professionalism had attracted growing donor scrutiny. Despite mounting social and economic needs, Uganda's defence spending as a percentage of GDP continued to rise, prompting concerns among international financial institutions such as the World Bank and the International Monetary Fund (IMF).[4] Uganda's major donors argued that the country was prioritizing salaries for redundant soldiers and expensive weapon purchase over key investments in health, education, and infrastructure. As a result, the World Bank and IMF conditioned their financial assistance on reductions in defence spending, urging the Ugandan government to bring its military budget down to 2% of Gross Domestic Product (GDP). This provoked strong resistance from the NRM regime, who accused donors of disregarding Uganda's security concerns. The NRM government justified high military expenditure as essential for maintaining internal peace and stability—conditions it argued were necessary to attract trade and investment. President Museveni warned that reducing defence spending would jeopardize citizens' security, particularly in northern Uganda, where the UPDF was still engaged in fighting LRA rebels.

The government further justified its position by portraying Uganda as surrounded by hostile neighbours—Congo, Sudan, and Kenya—who had refused to support the NRA's liberation struggle. In this context, reducing military expenditure was seen as a dangerous gamble. The UPDF political commissar explains that:

The donors, particularly the World Bank, were very wrong in forcing us to cut military spending and restructure our army. They forced us to retire many of our soldiers, thinking there won't be more wars. The outcomes were terrible for Uganda. You had many individuals who had spent their entire lives in the military being sent home without any retirement package. The result was prolonged insurgencies like the LRA and ADF because we ran short of manpower.[5]

Mid this tension, the government framed Uganda as a fragile state in need of donor assistance, not only for development but also for rebuilding its security infrastructure. In response, a national defence review was launched between June 2002, with funding from the UK's Department for International Development (DFID). Led by the Ministry of Defence, the review involved actors from across government, parliament, academia, and civil society. The process was overseen by the Defence Reform Secretariat and key regime figures, including President Museveni, Defence Minister Amama Mbabazi, Deputy Minister Ruth Nankabirwa, Army Commander Gen. Aronda Nyakairima, and Chief of Staff Maj. Gen. Joshua Masaba.[6]

Supporters of the defence review argued that the political instability Uganda faced from 1966 to 1986 had left the defence sector in disarray. Soldiers had been displaced, records destroyed, and operational structures severely weakened.[7] Rebuilding the military infrastructure required new foundations rooted in meritocracy, transparency, and accountability. Furthermore, the NRA's post-war structure and ideological orientation were considered outdated—still shaped by its guerrilla origins.[8] Soldiers routinely interacted with civilians in ways that are reflective of their wartime mindset, undermining the peace and stability the regime claimed to uphold. Thus, the goal was to transform the UPDF from a partisan, guerrilla-oriented force into a modern, professional, and accountable national military. This required upgrading both the "hardware" and "software" of the defence sector—investing not only in weapons and logistics but also in reshaping the attitudes, values, and institutional culture of the armed forces.

The review identified major weaknesses in Uganda's military institutions. Years of political crises—from 1966 to 1986—had devastated the country's military infrastructure. Operational systems were disorganized, personnel records were lost, and professional standards were virtually non-existent. From the bush, the NRA brought with it a guerrilla culture characterized by informality, loyalty-based promotions, and a highly personalized chain of command. These features, while useful during the bush war, became obstacles in peacetime as the regime struggled to transform the NRA into a professional national army.

The defence review recommended restructuring the military to align with principles of meritocracy, transparency, and accountability. This included re-sizing the force, enhancing oversight, and building systems for financial accountability and procurement. Training programs were introduced to instill discipline and encourage soldiers to adopt a professional military ethos—one rooted in service to the state, not loyalty to individuals or ethnic networks.

Yet, despite these intentions and donor backing, the reform process remained shaped by regime interests. While technical efficiency and professional capacity were improved, the army's political subordination to the presidency remained intact. The UPDF continued to function less as a neutral institution and more as a personalized instrument of regime consolidation, ensuring regime dominance rather than serving as a guarantor and protector of democracy.

Post-Defence Review Military Reforms

The Defence Review process culminated in the Defence White Paper, which laid the foundation for an ambitious effort to professionalize the UPDF. This document outlined national security priorities, mapped out a strategy for procurement and spending, and proposed reforms to eliminate inefficiencies while prioritizing resources toward emerging threats.

Significantly, it also created space for international donors to engage with and support Uganda's evolving defence agenda.[9]

> One of the most significant reforms was the structural re-organization of the Ugandan army. The first phase focused on rebuilding internal systems and transforming the NRA into the UPDF—a force envisioned to reflect Uganda's geographical and ethnic diversity. A major initiative involved downsizing the army from 60,000 to 48,000 soldiers to reduce fiscal pressure, improve training, and enhance operational readiness. Demobilized personnel were transferred to a reserve force, which remained under close surveillance to avoid potential involvement in destabilizing activities.

The Defence Review identified six major national security threats: border insecurity (including illicit trade and illegal crossings), destabilizing external influences from neighbouring states, internal political instability linked to weak institutions and contested governance, environmental degradation and resource competition, social polarization, and civil disasters. These threats informed the government's long-term strategic posture and guided subsequent security sector reforms.

To align its structure with these threats, the UPDF was divided into service branches—initially the Land Forces and the Air Force, later joined by the Reserve Force and the elite Special Forces Command (SFC). Within these branches, additional specialized units were established, including the infantry, artillery, armored brigades, engineering corps, air defense, logistics battalions, and medical units. These divisions were strategically deployed to cover all regions of Uganda: the 1st Division in Kakiri (central region), 2nd Division in Mbarara (west), 3rd Division in Moroto (east and Karamoja), and 4th Division in Gulu (north and West Nile). Each division is commanded by a senior officer and supported by intelligence units and military judicial structures like the divisional court martial.

In addition to structural reforms, the White Paper called for a $64 million investment to transition the Uganda People's Defence Forces (UPDF) from a conscription-based force to a professional, merit-based military. This investment encompassed the procurement of military hardware and the implementation of training initiatives. For instance, it recommended acquiring four inshore patrol vessels to secure Lake Victoria and the River Nile, alongside a $332,000 allocation for training marine units to operate the crafts.[10] In practice, the UPDF exceeded this target, procuring eight vessels and establishing a functional marine force. As a result, Uganda's waterways remain relatively secure despite persistent instability in neighboring South Sudan and the Democratic Republic of Congo.[11]

The review also advised strengthening air support capabilities through the acquisition of attack helicopters to bolster future infantry operations. However, the modernization of Uganda's air force has largely stalled. The UPDF continues to rely on six aging MiG-24 helicopters, three of which were lost in a 2012 crash over Mount Kenya while an route to Somalia for an African Union mission. Attempts to secure compensation from the United Nations were unsuccessful, as the helicopters had not yet reached the deployment zone at the time of the accident. A 2012 report by the International Institute for Strategic Studies described Uganda's air force as weak. Beyond the MiG-24 s, the UPDF maintains a fleet of seven reconditioned MiG-21s—one of which was lost in a 2008 crash that killed the pilot. Most of the fleet remains in poor condition and is widely considered non-operational.[12]

Although the White Paper offered a clear framework for rationalizing defence expenditure, the government has at times acted outside its recommendations. In 2011–2012, Uganda controversially purchased six Sukhoi Su-30MK2 fighter jets from Russia for $740 million. The transaction, conducted without prior parliamentary approval, sparked public outcry over the diversion of funds from critical sectors like health and education.[13] The executive later sought retroactive approval, prompting sharp criticism from lawmakers. Opposition MP Oduman Okello described the move as "insanity," condemning the government for prioritizing military hardware over essential public services.[14]

Despite mounting criticism, the government defended the military procurement program, citing regional instability, particularly in eastern Democratic Republic of Congo and South Sudan, and the need to safeguard strategic oil reserves in the Albertine Graben. Some of the threats outlined in the White Paper, including cross-border incursions, insurgent activity, and the risk of conflict with hostile states such as Sudan, provided a degree of justification for modernization efforts.[15] However, the opaque nature of the procurement process raised serious concerns about transparency, accountability, and fiscal discipline.

Internally, the government is acutely aware that Uganda's shifting political landscape may pose future challenges to regime stability. The prospect of a post-Museveni transition looms large, with potential to trigger political uncertainty and elite fragmentation. These dynamics have likely reinforced the regime's reliance on a loyal, well-resourced military. Moreover, Uganda's active role in regional peacekeeping—especially its deployment in Somalia under the African Union—has allowed the regime to both justify high defence spending and attract donor resources through military training and capacity-building initiatives.

Impact of the Strategic Defence Review

Since the completion of the Strategic Defence Review, Uganda has allocated substantial resources to a wide range of initiatives aimed at professionalizing and modernizing the military. These efforts included enhancing the capacity of intelligence agencies, establishing a reserve force, and creating Local Defence Units (LDUs) embedded in communities. The UPDF also expanded its regional role, increasingly engaging in conflict intervention and resolution efforts across East and Central Africa. Domestically, the government pledged to maintain a well-trained and well-equipped force capable of responding to sudden threats such as insurgencies, while also investing in preventive measures to mitigate them.

As proposed in the defence review, new institutional frameworks were established to improve coordination and oversight. The most notable among these are the Joint Intelligence Committee (JIC) and the National Security Council (NSC), both created in 2003 to streamline the army's command and control systems. The NSC, chaired by the president, comprises senior officials from the Ministries of Defence, the Security ministry, Internal Affairs, Foreign Affairs, and the Office of the Attorney General. It also included all heads of major security organs—including the Inspector General of Police, the Chief of Defence Forces, and the directors of the Internal and External Security Organizations (ISO and ESO). The NSC is responsible for advising the president on national security matters and coordinating intelligence assessments and recommendations produced by the JIC.

At the sub-national level, the defence review led to the formation of new structures such as District Security Committees (DSC), District Intelligence Committees (DIC), and Sub-County Security Committees (SSCs). These bodies, typically headed by military intelligence officers, extend military influence deep into the local governance system—strengthening surveillance and reinforcing the regime's control over potential political dissent.

Another key outcome of the restructuring process was the demobilization of thousands of redundant soldiers, contributing to cost efficiency. Senior military officers maintain that the UPDF has become a more professional, well-trained, and well-equipped force capable of responding to Uganda's evolving security needs. The legal framework guiding the force has also been updated. The UPDF Act outlines clear guidelines for the recruitment, deployment, retirement, and remuneration, and defines the military's intended role as a non-partisan institution that is "national in character, patriotic, professional, disciplined, productive, and subordinate to civilian authority."[16]

The reorganization of the force into formal infantry and mechanized brigades has further enhanced its operational capabilities. The UPDF has undertaken successful military operations both within Uganda—particularly in the north and west—and beyond its borders, including in the Democratic Republic of Congo, Central African Republic, and South Sudan.[17] Internationally, the UPDF has gained recognition for its participation in peacekeeping missions in Somalia, South Sudan, DRC and the Central African Republic (CAR). Likewise, Uganda's active role in counterterrorism—especially under the U.S.-led "war on terror"—has endeared the UPDF to Western donors, who now view Uganda as a key security partner and have generously supported its defence budget.[18]

While the UPDF's internal restructuring and enhanced capacity are evident, a critical question remains: Has the army transitioned, as envisioned in the White Paper, from a guerrilla movement into a non-partisan national army that embodies the collective interests and aspirations of Ugandans? The evidence suggests otherwise. Despite formal institutional reforms, the UPDF continues to serve as a key pillar of regime survival. Its role in the domestic political arena, particularly in suppressing opposition and safeguarding the status quo—reveals the persistence of partisan, personalized control of the military.

The personalization of command structures and the selective promotion of loyalists ensured that the UPDF remained firmly aligned with President Museveni's political objectives. Military deployments during election cycles, the use of elite units to suppress dissent, and the deliberate blurring of lines between national defense and internal repression illustrate how modernization was not purely professional or technical but deeply enmeshed in the authoritarian logic of regime durability. Thus, the UPDF remains both a national security institution and a political instrument—shaped by both Uganda's geostrategic environment and the internal calculations of power consolidation and regime continuity. The defence review led to substantial improvements—such as the creation of formal ranks, a code of conduct, and internal disciplinary structures—yet these reforms did little to dismantle the underlying culture of patronage and politicization. Loyalty to President Museveni and the NRM regime remained the principal determinant of advancement within the UPDF. Key positions continued to be dominated by individuals from Museveni's ethnic and political base, and military promotions often bypassed meritocratic procedures in favor of loyalty to the regime.

Therefore, despite the rhetoric of professionalization, the army has remained a pillar of regime survival. It is continuously used to intimidate political opposition, suppress dissent, and project state power in contested domains of power. As such, the UPDF is both a symbol and an instrument of the NRM's enduring authoritarian control. Moreover, the government used the reform agenda to rationalize rather than reduce military spending. Donors were assured that investments in modernization were necessary to professionalize the force, even as large portions of the defence budget remained opaque. Procurement scandals persisted, retirement packages for demobilized soldiers were poorly managed, and civil-military relations remained fraught.

Uganda's post–defence review military reforms reflect a hybrid approach—combining genuine institutional modernization with selective implementation tailored to serve regime interests. These reforms have been shaped by a dual logic: on one hand, the need to respond to credible external threats, such as cross-border insurgencies, regional instability in South Sudan and eastern Congo, and potential hostilities in the Great Lakes Region, provided a legitimate rationale for modernizing Uganda's army. On the other hand, internal imperatives of regime survival and political control significantly influenced how reforms were prioritized, funded, and operationalized.[19] The regime strategically directed military resources toward safeguarding critical regime assets—such as oil installations in the Albertine region—and reinforcing domestic political order through elite co-optation, intelligence expansion, and the militarization of internal security.

To fully grasp how the interests of military and political elites converge within the Museveni regime, it is necessary to examine the composition and underlying motivations of Uganda's ruling coalition. The subsequent sections show how, the top echelons of the military are disproportionately occupied by individuals from Museveni's inner circle—his relatives, longtime comrades from the Bush War, and loyalists from his ethnic and regional base. For this elite network, the survival of the regime is not only a political imperative but also a material necessity. The fear of losing access to state resources and patronage drives both political and military elites to resist any form of political transition that might jeopardize their wealth and privileges.

Personalization of the Army

When the NRA seized power in 1986, it established the National Resistance Council (NRC), initially composed of thirty-eight leading NRA political cadres and military elites. This body served as Uganda's first post-conflict parliament and was dominated by presidential appointees. In April 1987, the NRC was expanded to include cabinet ministers and their deputies, some of whom had not been part of the original NRA nucleus.[20] Though initially a militarized legislative body, this transformation was designed to portray the new government as more inclusive and representative than its predecessors.

In February 1989, a new legislation allowed further expansion of the NRC through elections and additional presidential appointments. This move was aimed at distancing the NRA government from Uganda's history of dictatorial regimes. Whereas Milton Obote's regime was dominated by northern elites and Idi Amin's by individuals from West Nile, the NRA positioned itself as a unifying force. Indeed, subsequent reforms accompanying the transformation of the NRA into the Uganda People's Defence Forces (UPDF) sought to create a more inclusive and professional military institution.

Efforts to diversify the UPDF have yielded mixed results. While there has been notable ethnic inclusion within the lower and middle ranks of the army, the upper echelons of military leadership remain heavily dominated by individuals from President Museveni's home region of western Uganda. Every officer who reached the rank of full General—the highest military rank— between 2000 and 2018, hailed from the west.[21] These included President Museveni himself; his brother, Gen. Caleb Akandwanaho (also known as Salim Saleh); Gen. David Tinyefuza (later Sejusa); Gen. Elly Tumwine; and Gen. Aronda Nyakairima, who died in 2015. Facing growing public criticism over this regional imbalance, Museveni promoted Gen. Jeje Odongo—a figure from outside his ethnic base—to the rank of full General in 2010. However, Odongo was immediately retired from the army following his promotion, a move widely interpreted as a calculated effort to neutralize his influence within the military hierarchy. Similarly, the elevation of Moses Ali, a retired officer from the West Nile sub-region to the same rank was largely symbolic. Given that Ali was no longer active in the military, the promotion was perceived as politically expedient rather than indicative of a meaningful shift toward inclusivity in senior military leadership.

In the early years of his rule, Museveni frequently articulated his vision for a new Ugandan army, one that would form the backbone of national democratization and socio-economic transformation.[22] He insisted that the military's role extended beyond warfighting and included contributing to internal development. Museveni argued that, once peace and stability were secured, the army would disengage from politics and permit democratic institutions to flourish.[23] Indeed, during the first fifteen years of his presidency, the military displayed notable discipline and restraint, earning praise from many Ugandans who saw this as a departure from the violent legacies of coups and military takeovers under previous regimes.[24]

Museveni was particularly critical of earlier governments for personalizing the army and failing to subordinate it to civilian control. In his memoir, he writes that, "in the past armies belonged to individuals and not to Uganda. We believe that armies should be national and nationalist. They should not be swept away by the changes of the government or by the exit of individuals from power."[25] Yet, despite these proclamations, Museveni's actions have increasingly mirrored the very tendencies he once condemned. Rather than building a professional and non-partisan military accountable to citizens, he has steadily personalized the UPDF and embedded it within the architecture of the ruling NRM party.

Two key dynamics underscore the personalization of the army under President Museveni's rule: First, the centralization of military control around the presidency and the deliberate politicization of the officer corps. Museveni has never fully disentangled himself from the military. He sees the UPDF as a direct product of his insurgent struggle and thus regards it not as an independent institution but as an extension of his personal legacy and regime authority. This perception has shaped how the army is managed: promotions, deployments, and key appointments are tightly controlled by the president and are often based on loyalty to Museveni himself, rather than professional competence or institutional performance. The military hierarchy is populated by individuals drawn from his inner circle, ethnic base, and bush war comrades, ensuring that the army's top leadership remains personally invested in regime survival.

Second, Museveni has actively blurred the line between the UPDF and the ruling NRM party, effectively transforming the military into a partisan institution. Despite constitutional and statutory provisions that define the UPDF as a non-partisan national force subordinate to civilian authority, the reality tells a different story. Senior officers regularly participate in political mobilization activities, speak in defense of government policies, and—during elections—play an outsized role in supporting the president. Many have been seen attending NRM rallies, providing logistical support to the party, and publicly denouncing opposition leaders.

Political patronage has further deepened the politicization of Uganda's military. Top-ranking officers are routinely rewarded with lucrative business opportunities, government appointments, and privileged access to state resources. Many senior officers now straddle both military and civilian roles—serving as ministers, ambassadors, or heads of key parastatal institutions—thus blurring the boundary between professional military service and civilian governance. These dual roles not only undermine the institutional autonomy of the army but also entrench officers' personal and financial interests in the continuity of President Museveni's regime. For example, Gen. Edward Katumba Wamala, the late Gen. Aronda Nyakairima, and Gen. David Muhoozi have all served in cabinet-level ministerial positions while still officially enlisted in the army. Their appointments reflect a deliberate strategy to embed military elites within civilian structures of power, reinforcing the fusion of military and political authority. Meanwhile, other figures like Gen. Salim Saleh—Museveni's brother—operate without any formal public office but wield extraordinary influence behind the scenes. Saleh's informal authority is so expansive that many regard him as the second most powerful figure in the country, often acting as a shadow policymaker, power broker, and dispenser of patronage.

In addition, there is enough evidence to suggest that promotions and appointments in the UPDF is not necessarily based on merit. The informal yet dominant criterion appears to be an individual's loyalty to President Museveni and the ruling NRM party. This logic of selection implies that the president must constantly surveil and assess the loyalty of his top lieutenants—determining who deserves advancement and who should be sidelined, purged, or rendered redundant due to perceived disloyalty. Uganda's tumultuous history, marked by military officers overthrowing political leaders, has made Museveni especially wary of independent-minded officers. As a result, loyalty and personal trust—not competence or performance—have become the currency of military advancement.

To ensure regime security, Museveni has consistently turned to a trusted network composed largely of his blood relatives, tribesmen, and comrades from the 1981–1986 bush war.[26] In doing so, transparency and meritocracy have been sacrificed at the altar of tribalism and nepotism. A 2008 survey conducted by *The Independent* magazine revealed that 75% of the top 23 military positions were occupied by officers from Museveni's home region of western Uganda. This regional dominance extends far beyond the apex of the hierarchy: central Uganda, the country's most populous region, held just 17% of these posts; northern Uganda 9%; and eastern Uganda none.[27]

Museveni has repeatedly attempted to justify this imbalance by pointing to the historical roots of the NRA insurgency, claiming that his early recruits were mostly from his ethnic group and geographic region.[28] Yet such explanations do not withstand serious scrutiny. On the contrary, Museveni has continued to entrench these disparities, seemingly viewing them as essential for his political survival. He continues to rely on a small circle of loyalists—often blood relatives and in-laws—for critical roles in army, including intelligence gathering, strategic planning, and covert assignments. These individuals serve not just as military officers but as regime gatekeepers.

This pattern has produced a military that, while nominally national in character, is substantively tied to narrow regional and familial interests. More broadly, it illustrates how Museveni's regime has deliberately personalized and politicized the army to reinforce regime stability rather than build inclusive, professional governance structures.[29] This web of patronage not only blurs institutional lines but also binds senior officers to the political survival of the president. Their wealth, status, and access to state power are directly tied to the durability of Museveni's rule. As a result, many within the military elite have become active participants in preserving the regime rather than remaining neutral guarantors of national security.

The Special Forces Command and the Politicization of Intelligence

President Museveni has often claimed that the idea of forming a small, specialized military unit dates back to his guerrilla days. During the bush war, it became difficult to conceal the movements of large groups—those exceeding 200 fighters. In response, he created small units such as Kabaleega (Kapeeka), Mondlane (Makulubita), Abdul Nasser (Matugga), and Nkrumah (Bukomero-Lukoola-Kyankwanzi). One particularly mobile unit was tasked with escorting the Chairman of the High Command—effectively acting as his personal protection detail. After the NRA seized power in 1986, this unit evolved into the Presidential Protection Unit (PPU), later transformed into the Presidential Guard Brigade (PGB), which grew to an estimated 10,000 to 15,000 soliders.

In 2010, Museveni merged the PGB with another elite army formation to create the Special Forces Command (SFC), placing it under the leadership of his son, Muhoozi Kainerugaba, with his cousin Sabiiti Magyenyi as deputy. This meant that the most skilled, best-trained, and best-equipped section of the army—including commandos, paratroopers, artillery, and infantry—was now under the command of the President's son. Beyond earning reasonably good salaries, SFC soldiers enjoy unique privileges not afforded to regular UPDF troops, including better welfare, improved housing and feeding, higher deployment allowances, and the ability to travel to their home villages while armed.

Initially tasked with protecting the President, the SFC's mandate expanded to include combat operations. In line with this elevation, Muhoozi was then promoted from brigadier to major general, reinforcing the notion that his rise was tied not to merit but to dynastic positioning within the military hierarchy. Although the 2004 Defense Review formally recognized only the Air Force and Land Forces as autonomous service branches, the expansion of the SFC effectively created a third service force which was officially recognized in 2025 following the amendment of the UPDF Act.

The SFC now plays a pivotal role in Uganda's internal security. It is frequently deployed to suppress anti-government protests, manages surveillance systems, protects strategic installations such as oil fields, and collects intelligence on both regime opponents and internal dissenters within the ruling party. Some political observers suggest that Uganda's most significant security threat during a post-Museveni transition may not stem from the regular army (UPDF), but from the SFC, which is dominated by personnel from Museveni's ethnic group and home region. Speaking about the process of recruitment to SFC, one observer remarked how one "cannot join SFC unless they have passed a strict vetting process" that includes "state agents coming to their villages, then to their families to collect information about political views and ethnicity."[30]

Although critics rightly highlight the dangers of family and ethnic-based recruitment, this strategy serves Museveni's consolidation of power in multiple ways. First, it ensures a cadre of military elites whose political and economic fortunes are intimately tied to the regime's survival. Second, by embedding blood ties into military command, Museveni fosters cohesion and preempts insubordination. For many within the SFC, a threat to the regime is a personal and communal threat, which makes them more willing to use force against perceived regime opponents without questioning the legitimacy or legality of their actions.

Unlike the SFC, recruitment into the regular army follows a more transparent, quota-based system, with district-level allocations proportional to population size. Military officials are eager to showcase ethnic and regional representation within the UPDF, citing the district-level recruitment structure as evidence of national inclusivity.[31] However, the dominance of Museveni's allies in senior command positions belies these claims. Notably, when asked about the ethnic composition or size of the SFC, officers refuse to disclose the data, citing national security concerns. This silence reflects the sensitivity surrounding the force's role and structure—and its centrality to regime consolidation.

In addition to the Special Forces Command (SFC), Uganda's intelligence agencies have become a central instrument of regime control, reinforcing the militarization of governance under President Museveni. Agencies such as the Chieftaincy of Military Intelligence (CMI), the Internal Security Organization (ISO), and the External Security Organization (ESO) operate not merely as technical arms of the state but as political tools embedded within Museveni's personalized security architecture.[32] Although their mandates differ—military intelligence, domestic surveillance, and foreign intelligence, respectively—their activities increasingly converge around protecting the regime rather than the republic.[33] These agencies bypass formal bureaucratic oversight and report directly to the President, allowing him to neutralize internal dissent, monitor political opponents, and suppress opposition mobilisazation.[34] Their growing prominence reflects a broader trend in Uganda's political landscape—i.e., the blurring of lines between national security and regime security, in which intelligence and coercive institutions are not just militarized in function but politicized in purpose.

As opposition to Museveni has intensified, these intelligence agencies have become increasingly active in surveillance, detention, and torture. They operate clandestine facilities—referred to as "safe houses"—where detainees are held incommunicado and tortured.[35] A 2009 Human Rights Watch (HRW) report documented widespread abuse, including mutilation, suspension from ceilings, beatings, and electrocution.[36] A former UN special rapporteur recounted: "We wrote a report documenting killings and torture. We insisted that Summit View in Kololo was a safe house and gave notice of a planned visit. They denied it, took us around, and showed us only offices. On our way out, someone whispered that there was a dungeon below where prisoners had been moved ahead of our visit."[37]

Opposition politicians frequently report being detained, interrogated, and tortured by agents from Uganda's key intelligence agencies. A particularly harrowing account comes from Francis Atugonza, the former mayor of Hoima city and a member of the opposition Forum for Democratic Change (FDC), who was arrested in 2009 and held incommunicado by the Joint Anti-Terrorism Task Force (JATF). Describing his ordeal, Atugonza recounted: "They beat me, tied my legs to the roof, and left me hanging upside down. They wanted to know where Besigye was getting money. When I said opposition activity is lawful, they beat me until I lost consciousness. They only took me to a hospital when they realized I might die."[38] His testimony, like many others, reveals how intelligence agencies—meant to protect the state—have been repurposed into instruments of political repression, targeting opposition figures with impunity in defense of regime survival.

Museveni's heavy reliance on intelligence agencies to suppress both internal dissent within the ruling party and external opposition underscores his insistence on absolute loyalty from their directors. The case of Amama Mbabazi illustrates how these agencies are deployed not only against the opposition, but also to neutralize potential challengers within the President's inner circle. As Security Minister and Secretary-General of the ruling National Resistance Movement (NRM), Mbabazi wielded considerable influence and was rumored to operate a "shadow state" through his control of key intelligence organs.[39] When speculation emerged that he harbored presidential ambitions, Museveni swiftly removed him from his security portfolio and reassigned him as Prime Minister—an ostensibly prestigious role but one with less control over the state coercive apparatus.[40] Despite this repositioning, leaked intelligence recordings—including interviews conducted by then Inspector General of Police Kale Kayihura—revealed that Mbabazi was quietly mobilizing support for a possible 2016 presidential bid.[41] The regime responded with urgency: Kayihura oversaw the interrogation of suspected Mbabazi loyalists and directed surveillance operations aimed at discrediting him. These efforts culminated in leaked tapes, which prompted the regime to prosecute whistleblowers and seek court injunctions to prevent further publication.[42] In an attempt to delegitimize Mbabazi, Museveni publicly accused him of spreading false rumors about a supposed succession plan involving his son, Muhoozi Kainerugaba. "I sacked Mbabazi because he went around the country saying I was preparing my son Muhoozi to become president," Museveni stated. "My son has never even stood for LC1, and the Constitution is very clear on how one can be elected President."[43] When Mbabazi ultimately declared his candidacy, he was kicked out of NRM's National Executive Committee (NEC), labeled a traitor, and the NRM swiftly amended party rules to block his nomination, ensuring that Museveni remained the sole candidate.

The Mbabazi experience reveals the extent to which Uganda's intelligence and security apparatus has been reconfigured into a mechanism for preserving the NRM regime. Intelligence agencies, far from being neutral state institutions, function as extensions and guarantees of the regime hegemony—mobilized not only to silence external dissent but also to preempt and dismantle internal power centres that might pose a threat to the regime. The orchestration of surveillance, political purges, and legal maneuvering to eliminate Mbabazi's challenge demonstrates that loyalty, not institutional procedure, determines who thrives within the system. These dynamic underscores the deeper structural transformation of Uganda's coercive institutions. They do not serve the state in the traditional sense but are embedded in a militarized and highly personalized governance system where the boundary between state security and regime security is effectively fused.

The Uganda Police as a Quasi-Military Organization

Historically, the Uganda Police Force was a civilian institution led by professional police officers. However, in 2001, President Yoweri Museveni appointed then-Major General Katumba Wamala, a serving senior military officer, as Inspector General of Police (IGP). This marked a significant departure from tradition and coincided with the 2001 presidential elections. As overall commander of the police, Wamala superintended security during the electoral period. Under his leadership, the police routinely disrupted opposition rallies, particularly in rural areas considered to be strongholds of Museveni's regime.[44]

In contrast to the 1996 general elections—during which the police largely maintained neutrality—the 2001 elections witnessed the Uganda Police's first overtly partisan intervention in favor of the ruling NRM party. Despite these developments, Wamala was credited with limiting the scale of electoral violence. In the aftermath, concerns about the neutrality of the police grew among the public.[45] In response, Wamala launched a series of community engagement initiatives aimed at rebuilding trust. His approach yielded some internal reforms, shifting police attitudes and operations in ways that led many to view his efforts as genuine. This optimism led to speculation that the 2006 elections might be more peaceful.

However, ahead of the 2006 polls, Museveni made a surprise reshuffle and reassigned Wamala military duties and appointed General Kale Kayihura—another military officer—as his replacement. Kayihura had previously commanded the UPDF's notorious Anti-Smuggling Unit and had served as operational commander during the UPDF's controversial campaign in the Ituri province of the DRC in 1998. In addition to Kayihura's appointment, new military officers were placed in charge of key police units, including the now-defunct Special Branch, the Narcotics Division, the Intelligence Unit, and the Rapid Response Unit—all closely aligned with regime interests.[46]

After taking charge of the police, Kayihura introduced controversial changes aimed at positioning the police as a central actor in Uganda's contentious political landscape. He dismissed or demoted seasoned police officers, recruited thousands of new personnel, and promoted individuals known to be loyal to the regime.[47] He also created or revitalized several specialized units—such as the Anti-Terrorism Unit, the Rapid Response Unit, the Police Standards Unit, the Political Crimes Unit, and the Flying Squad Unit.[48] Many of these units were staffed by former UPDF soldiers, raising serious concerns about the professional orientation of the force. As the Uganda Human Rights Commission noted, these soldiers were trained for combat, not policing.[49] This blurring of roles led to a sharp rise in civilian deaths at the hands of security forces. These units became instrumental in the arrest, detention, torture and harassment of opposition and human rights activists. In suppressing anti-regime mobilisation, the police—under these militarized units—appear to operate with a "shoot first, ask questions later" doctrine.[50] As a result, it became increasingly difficult to distinguish police and military actions. Military operations were often disguised as police work, with soldiers wearing police uniforms. This lack of distinction led to widespread human rights abuses by army officers in police uniforms. According to Nicholas Opiyo, head of Chapter Four-Uganda, a Kampala-based human rights organization, most torture victims he assisted were abused by military officers embedded within the police. He explains that "sometimes it is difficult to ascertain whether it is the police or UPDF engaged in torture. When the UPDF do torture, they dump their victims at police stations when they are about to die. So, the police bear the burden... If you go to room six at Kampala Central Police Station (KCPS); it is run by the soldiers. They dump their victims after they have beaten them. And they leave police to face the burden and the blame."[51]

Beyond embedding military officers within the Ugandan police, Kayihura expanded the size and reach of the police directorates, transforming the force into a more centralized and politically responsive instrument of regime control. Initially, this expansion raised hopes that increased police presence would improve public safety and protect civil liberties. However, these expectations were soon dashed. In many regions, especially in northern Uganda—where the UPDF was battling the LRA rebels—residents could not distinguish between police and military personnel. Military officers often operated police posts, blurring institutional boundaries. A 2007 report by the UN High Commissioner for Human Rights criticized this fusion of roles, warning that it had eroded public confidence in the police and undermined the civilian nature of law enforcement.[52]

The extent of police militarization under Kayihura since 2005 is unmatched in Uganda's post-colonial history. The police's conduct during the 2006, 2011, and 2016 elections—marked by violence, repression, and arbitrary arrests—suggests that Museveni endorsed Kayihura's approach. The police was tasked not only with maintaining order but also with persecuting opposition figures, conducting surveillance, enforcing repressive legislation, and executing orders that undermine constitutional freedoms. One particularly controversial oppressive law was the Public Order Management Act (POMA), which grants the police sweeping powers to approve or deny public gatherings. While organizers of social and cultural events easily receive police clearance, opposition mobilisation events were routinely blocked. POMA become a blueprint for repression, used to suppress dissent and restrict freedom of assembly. Both Museveni and Kayihura championed this law, framing it as a necessary measure for maintaining security and public order.

These restrictions often violate Uganda's constitutional protections. Article 29 guarantees freedom of conscience, expression, assembly, and association.[53] Yet the police regularly violate these rights, often citing vague "orders from above" to justify their actions. Some human rights activists contend that blame should be directed not at the rank-and-file officers—many of whom lack training or act under duress, but at the regime's leadership.[54] Margaret Sekajja, former UN country rapporteur and current executive director of the Human Rights Centre, has conducted several human rights training sessions with police personnel. She remains frustrated by the leadership's unwillingness to implement what officers have learned. She reveals that "many of these officers are lawyers. They clearly understand human rights and the role they are expected to play. When you question their brutal conduct, they give you one excuse: 'We are just following orders from above'. You are left wondering who's that 'above' that gives these irrational orders."[55]

As political opposition to Museveni's rule intensifies, the position of IGP became increasingly politicized. Under the 2003 Police Act, the President appoints the IGP—effectively ensuring the role is occupied by an individual loyal to him. Museveni has consistently prioritized loyalty over competence. One MP explains that appointment of the IGP is "all about who can serve better the interests of an individual hell-bent on keeping himself in power at all costs."[56]

Despite mounting public pressure and numerous petitions demanding Kayihura's removal, Museveni continually renewed his contract. Kayihura openly dismissed critics, insisting that he merely executes the President's directives.[57] At one point, he stated that "those who have been saying Kayihura is militarizing police, it's in the law. This is just the beginning… I found police with SAR (semi-automatic rifles), now they have SMGs (sub-machine guns), they now have anti-aircraft machine guns. I am now going to buy them Saba Saba (cannons). Why not? This is an order from the President."[58]

The result of embedding military officers in top police positions is the erosion of institutional boundaries between military and police forces.[59] Although these agencies are formally distinct, in practice they operate as a unified force, answering to the same command structure. This dynamic reflects the regime's enduring "bush war mentality"—a view in which militarized solutions are applied to every form of political contestation.[60] As one activist remarked:

> Museveni believes that the military is a solution to Uganda's problems. That's why you see the military dominating every institution of the state. The police (are) headed by a general who has never had any training in policing. He believes in military power first, not police. This is the same belief the President holds. That's why each time the President wants to make a serious statement he has first to wear his military uniform.[61]

This analysis underscores the intricate networks of power within Museveni's regime, where the police institution functions as a central pillar of an informal system of governance. The Police Statute of 1994 formally places the Inspector General of Police (IGP) under the authority of the Ministry of Internal Affairs yet, in practice, the IGP operates under the direct influence of the President. This deviation from formal procedure undermines ministerial oversight and embeds the police within a highly personalized structure of executive power. Crucially, this pattern is not unique to the police—it reflects a broader trend that permeates other security organs, further entrenching authoritarian control through militarized and informal channels.

Notes

1. Rubongoya, J. (2007) *Regime Hegemony in Museveni's Uganda: Pax Musevenica*, pp. 181. New York: Palgrave Macmillan.
2. Tangri, R., & Mwenda, A. M. (2007) 'Military Corruption & Ugandan Politics since the Late 1990's' *Review of African Political Economy,* 30: 98, 2003, pp. 539–552.
3. Darryl T. C., and Mazrui A (1992) "Africa's Post-Cold War Demilitarization: Domestic and Global Causes." *Journal of International Affairs*, vol. 46, no. 1 pp. 157–174.

4. Tangri, R., & Mwenda, A. M. (2003). Military corruption & Ugandan politics since the late 1990s. *Review of African Political Economy*, 30(98), 539–552. https://doi.org/10.1080/02.
5. Interview with Col. Felix Kulayigye. ibid.
6. Uganda Government White Paper on Defence Transformation, June 2004.
7. Hendrickson D. (2007) (ed.) *Uganda Defence Review: Learning From Experience*, Kings College, London, UK.
8. Interview with Hon. Muwanga Kivumbi, a Member of Parliament who sits on the Parliamentary Defence Committee (June 3, 2016).
9. Interview with Felix Kulayigye, Ibid.
10. Interview with Col. Ba-Hoku Barigye, UPDF deputy Political Commissar (July 17, 2016).
11. Interview with Col. Ba-Hoku Barigye. ibid.
12. IISS the Military Balance report, 2012.
13. Interview with Francis Mwijukye, MP for Buhweju constituency (May 12, 2015).
14. See the interview of shadow finance minister Oduman Okello as quoted Reuters by "Uganda opposition: govt wrong to buy Russia fighters" (April 7, 2011) Available online: http://www.reuters.com/article/uganda-jets-idAFLDE7361WA20110407.
15. Relief Web (1998) "Sudan Denies It Bombed Northern Uganda" (October 6) Available online: http://reliefweb.int/report/sudan/sudan-denies-it-bombed-northern-uganda.
16. The UPDF act 2005.
17. Fisher J. (2012) "Managing donor perceptions: Contextualizing Uganda's 2007 intervention in Somalia", *African Affairs*, Volume 111, Issue 444, July 2012, Pages 404–423.
18. Abrahamsen, R and Bareebe G., (2016) "Briefing: Uganda's 2016 Elections: Not Even Faking It Anymore." *African Affairs*, vol. 115, no. 461, pp. 751–65.
19. Interview with Nicholas Opio. Ibid.
20. Mudoola, D. M. 1(989) "Institution-Building: The Case of the NRM and the Military in Uganda, 1986–89." Paper presented at the Conference on Uganda: Structural Adjustment and Revolutionary Change (Lyngby Landsbrugsskole, Denmark.
21. International Crisis Group report, 2012.

22. Professionalizing the army has been a common topic in various speeches of Museveni available online: http://www.statehouse.go.ug.
23. Uganda State House Website http://www.statehouse.go.ug.
24. Oloka-Onyango J. (2004) "'New Breed' Leadership, Conflict, and Reconstruction in the Great Lakes Region of Africa: A Sociopolitical Biography of Uganda's Yoweri Kaguta Museveni", *Africa Today*, p. 29.
25. Museveni Y.K. (2000) "What is Africa's Problem?" Kampala.
26. Interview with Hon. Kaps Fungaroo, a Member of Parliament and former Shadow Minister for Defence.
27. The Independent, January 25, 2008.
28. Independent, March 11, 2009; *The Observer July 18, 2012; Daily Monitor July 18, 2012.*
29. Interview with Maj. John Kazoora, ibid.
30. Interview with Benard Sabiti. ibid.
31. Interview with Col. Ba-hoku Barigye. ibid.
32. Privacy International. ibid. p. 5.
33. Rwengabo, S. 2012, Ibid.
34. Rwengabo, S. 2012, Ibid.
35. Interview with a retired intelligence officer who did not want to be publicly identified.
36. Bareebe G. (2010) "Rights body blocked from Safe Houses" Daily Monitor (February 23), Kampala, Available online: http://www.monitor.co.ug/News/National/688334-866940-c9cav5z/index.html.
37. Interview with Margaret Sekajja.ibid.
38. Interview with Francis Atugonza, former Mayor of Hoima municipality and opposition fugure (August 17, 2017).
39. Chimpreports (2015) "Tumwebaze: Mbabazi was most powerful Minister in Museveni's cabinet" November 18,. Available http://www.chimpreports.com/tumwebaze-mbabazi-was-most-powerful-minister-in-musevenis-cabinet.
40. Daily Monitor (2012) "Museveni's attack on Mbabazi rocks NRM" June 21 Available online: http://www.monitor.co.ug/News/National/Museveni-s-attack-on-Mbabazi-rocks-NRM/688334-1431836-e8nbie/index.html.

41. NTV-Uganda (2014) "New Secret Kayihura Tapes Leak" April 15. Available online: https://www.youtube.com/watch?v=ouWS1X2bFB.
42. NTV-Uganda (2014) ibid.
43. Daily Monitor" (2015) "Museveni Hits Out at Mbabazi Over Muhoozi" November 5, Available online at: http://www.monitor.co.ug/News/National/Museveni-hits-out-at-Mbabazi-over-Muhoozi/688334-2944022-po3lp2z/index.htm.
44. Interview Tumwine Patrick.ibid.
45. Interview with Journalist Charles Odoobo-Bichachi. Ibid.
46. Rwengabo, Sabastiano (2012). Ibid.
47. Interview with Francis Mwijuke. Ibid.
48. Interview with Robert Ssempala ibid.
49. See, for example, a statement by Uganda Human Rights Commission. Available online http://uhrc.ug/uhrc-statement-recent-'shoot-kill'-order-uganda-police-force.
50. Interviews with Michael Kabaziguruka.ibid.
51. Interview with Nicholas Opio.ibid.
52. A report by the United Nations (UN) High Commissioner for Human Rights as reference in Human Watch report. Available online: https://www.hrw.org/legacy/english/docs/2007/05/21/uganda15971_txt.htm.
53. The Uganda Constitution 1995.
54. Interview with Robert Ssempala. ibdi.
55. Interview with Margaret Sekajja. Ibid.
56. Interview with Francis Mwijuke.ibid.
57. Also, see Privacy International, 2015, p. 6.
58. Daily Monitor, Ibid.
59. Interview with Margaret Sekajja.Ibid.
60. Interview with John Njoroge. ibid.
61. Patrick Tumwine. ibid.

CHAPTER 6

Visible but Powerless: Politics, Opposition, and Social Group Containment Under the NRM

From the Battlefield to the Ballot

Although President Museveni easily won the 1996 and 2001 general elections, he faced prolonged electoral battles with opposition leader Kizza Besigye in 2006, 2011, and 2016. Besigye's charisma, bravery, and willingness to challenge the regime's repressive tactics attracted millions to his presidential campaign. Many Ugandans who once thought that a Museveni defeat was improbable in 2001 began to see the possibility of a post-Museveni era.

One reason Museveni's early electoral victories were relatively uncontested is that Uganda was operating under a no-party system. Political parties had been effectively banned, with Museveni accusing them of having fueled the "sectarian divide" that previously destabilized the country.[1] These elections also took place during the early years of Museveni's rule, a period when he still enjoyed significant popular support following decades of conflict, misrule, and instability. Yet still, as Museveni further entrenched one-party rule, both internal dissent and external pressure—particularly from donor groups—mounted in favor of political liberalization. In 2000, a national referendum was held to determine whether Uganda should retain the no-party system or return to multiparty politics.[2] Although many Ugandans were poorly informed about the process and a significant portion of the population boycotted the vote,

G. Bareebe, *Social Structures and the Making of Museveni's Civil-Authoritarian Regime in Uganda*,
https://doi.org/10.1007/978-3-032-14015-9_6

the results signaled public support for a multiparty system. Consequently, the 2006 general elections marked the first time since 1980 that multiple political parties participated in both presidential and local council races.

The transition to multipartyism presented a significant challenge to the Ugandan army, which had long operated within a one-party framework. This challenge intensified in 2005, when President Museveni pushed through a controversial constitutional amendment that removed presidential term limits. The move triggered tensions within both the ruling NRM party and the military. Several former allies broke ranks, forming the Parliamentary Advocacy Forum (PAFO), which later aligned with Besigye's Reform Agenda (RA) platform. Besigye, who had contested the 2001 presidential election and rejected the results on grounds of electoral fraud, had fled into exile in South Africa, citing threats to his life.

In 2005, the PAFO and Reform Agenda (RA) merged to form the Forum for Democratic Change (FDC), with Kizza Besigye elected as its presidential flagbearer while still in exile. His return to Uganda galvanized a politically restless public eager for change. Besigye embarked on a nationwide consultative tour that drew massive crowds, reinvigorating opposition politics and raising widespread hopes for a democratic transfer of power. Within the regime, Besigye was seen as a formidable threat. His track record both in the army and in politics was impressive. He had served as commander of the mechanized brigade, chief of logistics and engineering, and national political commissar. During the guerrilla war, he was Museveni's personal physician, and following the NRM's ascent to power, he held a ministerial position in its first government. His insider status and revolutionary credentials lent credibility to his dissent, making him a uniquely dangerous challenger to Museveni's rule.

To counter Besigye's growing influence, Museveni turned to his most loyal institution—the military—and deployed the regime's intelligence apparatus to discredit Besigye's candidature. Central to this effort was the fabrication of a rebel group, the so-called People's Redemption Army (PRA), which regime officials claimed was operating out of eastern Congo under Besigye's command.[3] Although no credible evidence substantiated the group's existence, the regime weaponized this narrative to justify Besigye's arrest in October 2005 and his prosecution in a military court on treason charges—offenses that carried the death penalty.[4] In addition to the treason charges, Besigye was charged with rape in the High Court, accused of assaulting his housemaid on two separate occasions. His legal team argued that the allegations were politically motivated, designed to discredit him personally and neutralize his growing challenge to Museveni's rule. The timing and nature of the charges raised serious concerns about the instrumentalization of the judiciary for political ends.[5]

The regime, however, committed a procedural misstep by charging Besigye with the same offense—treason—in both the High Court and the court martial. This dual prosecution exposed tensions between Uganda's civilian judiciary and the military justice system. While the High Court signaled its intent to assert judicial independence, the state appeared to favor the court martial, where the executive wielded greater influence.[6] Besigye's legal team contested the court martial's jurisdiction, arguing that he had retired from the military in 2001 and was therefore a civilian, not subject to military trial.

The Constitutional Court unanimously ruled that Besigye could not be tried by a court martial, affirming his civilian status. In response, the High Court granted bail to him and 14 co-accused. However, as they attempted to leave the court premises, a heavily armed military unit stormed the courtroom and re-arrested them in a blatant display of executive defiance. Fearing torture or illegal detention, the accused refused to sign their bail papers, ensuring they remained in civilian court rather than military custody. The unit responsible for the raid was later identified as the 'Black Mambas Urban Hit Squad,' an auxiliary force linked to the Chieftaincy of Military Intelligence (CMI). Uganda's then Principal Judge, James Ogoola, condemned the military raid of the high court in stark terms, describing it as "a despicable act" and "a rape of the Court" and likened it to the lawlessness era of the Idi Amin.[7]

In response to the state's conduct, the Constitutional Court acquitted Besigye of all charges, declaring: "This court cannot sanction any continued prosecution of the petitioners where during the proceedings, their human rights have been violated. No matter how strong the evidence, a fair trial cannot be achieved, and any subsequent trials would be a waste of time and an abuse of court process."[8] Despite this unequivocal ruling, the state pressed forward with the rape charge—a move Besigye, and his legal team denounced as politically orchestrated to tarnish his reputation and taint his presidential candidacy. The High Court ultimately dismissed the case, concluding that the prosecution had failed to present credible evidence and that the investigation had been "crude and amateurish," reflecting its underlying political motives.[9] In a scathing judgment that underscored the politically motivated nature of the case, Justice John Bosco Katutsi wrote:

> The evidence before this court is inadequate even to prove a debt—impotent to deprive of a civil right—ridiculous for convicting of the pettiest offence—scandalous if brought forward to support a charge of any grave character—monstrous if to ruin the honour of a man who offered himself as a candidate for the highest office of this country.[10]

Justice Katutsi's ruling not only acquitted Besigye of rape and all other charges but also laid bare the political manipulation of state institutions—especially the police and the Criminal Investigations Department (CID), against opponents of President Museveni. The case exposed how these institutions are weaponized to suppress political opposition and tarnish Besigye's reputation by portraying him as a rapist, thereby undermining his challenge to Museveni's hold on power.

The UPDF as Guardians of the Throne

Ironically, President Museven, who once criticized past Ugandan regimes for using the military to suppress dissent, had come to rely on the very same tactics to consolidate power. To his credit, the military had largely stayed on the political periphery during the first decade of his rule. However, as political opposition mounted, Museveni increasingly leaned on the coercive capacities of the state, particularly after 2001.

The 2001 elections marked a turning point. While Museveni's victory was never in doubt, the regime's security apparatus appeared unwilling to tolerate sustained political competition. Military and intelligence units intervened selectively in regions where the opposition, particularly Besigye's Reform Agenda, was gaining traction.[11] Opposition supporters were arrested, often without charge, and subjected to harassment and intimidation—measures clearly intended to disrupt mobilization rather than eliminate the opposition outright.

Even within the military itself, dissent was discouraged. Retired officers were warned against supporting Besigye; those who resisted faced spurious charges or loss of benefits. A striking example was the case of Major Rwaboni Okwiri, a retired army officer and head of the Reform Agenda's youth desk. On February 20, 2001, Okwiri was violently arrested at Entebbe International Airport, beaten by plainclothes soldiers, and taken to CMI headquarters.[12] There, he was stripped and interrogated for six hours about the opposition's political networks and funding sources. He was released the following day, but only after being forced to publicly renounce his involvement in opposition politics under military supervision.[13]

Several other campaign officials—such as Hajji Ramathan Muwonge, Siraje Wamara, Kaamu Benjamin, Florence Mirembe Kitenda, and Godfrey Nsubuga—were arrested, tortured, and released without charges.[14] In Mbale, two opposition agents were killed by the military on January 21, 2001. A 2002 parliamentary inquiry concluded that the UPDF had played a direct role in election-related violence.[15]

By the 2006 elections, military interference had become more brazen. In one notorious incident, Lt. Ramathan Magara opened fire on Besigye supporters during a rally in Kampala, killing two and maiming others.[16] Beyond overt violence, military officers actively campaigned for Museveni and issued threats aimed at dissuading Ugandans from voting for the opposition. For instance, in 2001, Lt. Gen. Henry Tumukunde flew by helicopter to Rukungiri—Besigye's home district—where he publicly declared that he would never salute a President Besigye.[17] Coming from a serving army officer, this statement not only breached military codes of conduct and the Ugandan constitution,[18] but also highlighted the regime's willingness to tolerate, and even implicitly endorse, partisan behavior within the armed forces, so long as it was in support of the regime leader.

Ahead of the 2011 election, similar threats resurfaced. Army commander Gen. Aronda Nyakairima warned that the UPDF would "move decisively" against any attempts to protest Museveni's re-election.[19] The then Special Forces Commander Muhoozi Kainerugaba—Museveni's son—echoed this message, stating that the military would confront any groups seeking to "destabilize the country during the polls."[20] Such statements, though clearly unconstitutional, were not only tolerated but effectively rewarded. Officers who publicly supported the regime were often promoted or assigned lucrative deployments, reinforcing the logic of political loyalty within the military hierarchy.

The post-election *Walk-to-Work* protests of 2011 offer a revealing lens into the growing role of the military and intelligence agencies in sustaining the Museveni regime. Following the 2011 general elections, whose results were hotly contested by the opposition—demonstrations erupted in Kampala and other urban centers, with many Ugandans decrying electoral fraud and deteriorating socio-economic conditions. The state responded swiftly and brutally. Opposition leaders, including Kizza Besigye, were arrested multiple times and charged with organizing unlawful assemblies. Many of their supporters were rounded up and detained in undisclosed locations across the country.

The regime feared that the protests could spiral into an Egyptian-style uprising. In response, they launched a violent crackdown. Dozens of protesters were killed, many others maimed, and hundreds subjected to arbitrary detention. Military and intelligence agencies—including the Chieftaincy of Military Intelligence (CMI), Internal Security Organisation (ISO), External Security Organisation (ESO), and the Special Forces Command (SFC)—played central roles in suppressing the protests.[21] Armed operatives, often in civilian clothes and without identification, abducted suspected protest organizers, blindfolded them, and transported them in unmarked vehicles to CMI headquarters in Kitante.[22] There, detainees were interrogated and tortured for information about opposition planned activities.

While the regime's coercive machinery is primarily deployed against the opposition, it is also used to enforce discipline within the ruling party. In 2013, amid an internal NRM crisis sparked by parliamentary investigations into an oil bribery scandal implicating senior officials, Museveni warned that a military takeover was possible if "confusion" continued within the party.[23] Shortly thereafter, Gen. Nyakairima publicly warned MPs that the military would not tolerate "bad politics,"[24] a statement reinforced by then-Defence Minister Crispus Kiyonga, who said, "If the military feels the country is in the hands of wrong politicians, some officers might be forced to intervene in the name of refocusing the country's future."[25] Though many Ugandans dismissed these warnings as rhetorical bluster, the symbolism is clear: the military remained the ultimate guarantor of regime survival. Defence officials later confirmed that these statements were not isolated but reflected deliberate signaling from the President—signals that were, in their words, "well taken."[26]

It is thus clear that the Ugandan army and intelligence agencies, once seen as apolitical, have become deeply enmeshed in partisan politics, operating as the regime's primary enforcers. The army's involvement in acts of coercion, the manipulation of legal institutions, and overt threats of military intervention, shows that Museveni regime has institutionalized a model of authoritarian governance sustained by force rather than democratic legitimacy. This militarization of politics has not only eroded constitutional boundaries and civilian oversight but also reshaped the UPDF into a political actor that is now central to the regime's survival.

Military Power and the Containment of Residual Social Structures: The 2009 Buganda Protests

The 2009 Buganda protests offer a compelling case of the UPDF's instrumental role in safeguarding the Museveni regime and curbing the influence of Uganda's residual social structures—most notably, powerful traditional monarchies such as the Buganda Kingdom. As previously noted, after seizing power in 1986, President Museveni pledged to restore the traditional kingdoms that had been abolished during the Obote era.[27] However, their reinstatement soon generated tensions, as the interests of these revived institutions increasingly clashed with those of the NRM regime.

Among the restored institutions, the Buganda Kingdom—Uganda's most populous and economically dominant—initially served as a critical ally of the NRM regime. Museveni rewarded this support by sanctioning the restoration of monarchy in 1993 and overseeing the coronation of its Kabaka (King). Yet the alliance quickly deteriorated. The kingdom presented a set of demands to the central government, including a federal arrangement granting it autonomy, the return of 9,000 square miles of land under government control, and the withdrawal of state administrative structures from its territory.[28] The decentralization program—initiated in the 1980s and expanded throughout the 1990s—deepened this friction. Although it was ostensibly aimed to bring services closer to the people, Buganda officials perceived the creation of numerous districts as a deliberate "divide and rule" tactic, intended to fragment the kingdom and weaken its collective capacity for political mobilization.[29]

Tensions erupted into open conflict on September 10, 2009, when the government blocked the Kabaka from visiting Kayunga District. Though located within Buganda's historical boundaries, Kayunga is largely inhabited by the Banyara, a sub-ethnic community that had long agitated for autonomy from Buganda. Kingdom leaders accused the government of exploiting Banyara discontent to undermine Buganda's territorial authority. In 2008, with state backing, Banyara elders installed their own king, who was subsequently granted the same privileges as other recognized monarchs—an act perceived by Buganda as a calculated affront.

To assert its claim over Kayunga and counter the Banyara secessionist initiative, the Buganda Kingdom organized a visit by the Kabaka. The central government opposed the visit, arguing that the Kabaka should first obtain consent from Banyara elders. For Buganda monarchists, this condition was not only humiliating but also illegitimate, as it implied the Kabaka's authority did not extend across the kingdom's traditional territory.[30] A political standoff ensued, with many Baganda accusing President Museveni of orchestrating a divide-and-rule strategy to curtail the Kabaka's influence.[31]

When an advance team from the kingdom attempted to enter Kayunga to prepare for the Kabaka's visit, they were intercepted by a combined force of police and military units. News of this confrontation triggered spontaneous protests across Kampala and other parts of Buganda. More than any other traditional leader in Uganda, the Kabaka commands profound loyalty from his subjects and presides over his kingdom with the autonomy of a "state within a state," giving him substantial political leverage to challenge or negotiate with the central government.[32] The speed and scale of the protests—fueled by widespread grievances over perceived political marginalization—prompted the state to deploy a joint force comprising the Special Forces Command, units of the regular army, and the police.

The security response was brutal. Over the course of two days, more than 40 people were killed, at least 100 were injured, and 560 were arrested.[33] Footage broadcast on local television showed bodies lying in the streets as Special Forces troops—under the command of Museveni's son, Lt. Gen. Muhoozi Kainerugaba—used advanced assault weapons to suppress demonstrators. The government imposed a media blackout and issued gag orders banning radio and TV stations from reporting on the unrest. Those that defied the directive, including CBS (owned by the Buganda Kingdom), were forcibly shut down.[34]

In the aftermath, many Ugandans expressed outrage at the excessive force used by security agencies and demanded an investigation. While police initially pledged to investigate the killings, they later claimed they lacked the authority to investigate other security organs involved in the operation. The Speaker of Parliament tasked the Defence and Internal Affairs Committee to investigate and produce a report within two weeks, but MPs were denied access to key sites and witnesses. One legislator remarked, "The state doesn't want people to know what happened. And I am sure we will never know how such many people were killed in just two days of protests… I can assure you that the death toll is even higher. It is hard to know the truth because the media was blocked from reporting and radio stations were closed."[35]

The 2009 Buganda protests thus reveal not only the regime's readiness to deploy lethal force in containing influential traditional structures but also the broader strategy of controlling narratives, suppressing dissent, and fragmenting cohesive social formations that might challenge centralized state authority.

Military Power and the Containment of Residual Social Structures: The 2016 Rwenzururu Crisis

As in the case of Buganda, the Rwenzururu Kingdom—located in western Uganda near the border with the Democratic Republic of Congo—has a long-standing history of tension with the central government, dating back to the 1960s.[36] While the restoration of traditional kingdoms formed part of Museveni's broader strategy of co-optation, the Rwenzururu Kingdom presented an exceptional challenge. Unlike other reinstated monarchies, Rwenzururu carried a legacy of ethnic nationalism and armed resistance. Its traditional leaders, venerated as both cultural icons and political figures, had historically defied external domination, first resisting subjugation by the neighboring Tooro Kingdom, which was backed by the British colonial administration, and later opposing various post-independence regimes. Museveni's initial reluctance to recognize the Rwenzururu monarchy stemmed from concerns that its revival might galvanize separatist aspirations in an already restive and geopolitically sensitive region.

Despite his reservations, Museveni eventually bowed to sustained pressure from Rwenzururu monarchists and approved the formation of a restoration committee in 1999. Nevertheless, his hesitancy remained evident, reinforced by opposition from senior figures within the ruling NRM, including then-Defence Minister Crispus Kiyonga. The NRM's dismal performance in the Rwenzori region during the 2006 elections—widely attributed to the regime's delay in restoring the kingdom—compelled Museveni to reconsider his stance. In response, he lifted his objections, and in October 2009, Charles Wesley Mumbere was officially crowned Omusinga (King) of the Obusinga Bwa Rwenzururu.

Museveni's hope was to absorb Rwenzururu into his clientelist network—similar to arrangements with kingdoms like Tooro, Bunyoro, and Busoga. However, he underestimated the region's historical defiance and deep-seated resistance to external control. The Rwenzururu monarchy's foundation was born from armed resistance, and its self-determination ethos remained intact even after formal recognition. In the 1980s, for example, remnants of the kingdom formed the Rwenzururu Freedom Movement (RFM) to fight Obote's government, while other monarchs fled into exile.

Tensions with the central government re-emerged shortly after restoration. Disagreements escalated when the state sponsored a separate traditional leader for the Bamba sub-ethnic—widely perceived by Bakonzo elites as an effort to fracture and weaken Rwenzururu authority, echoing similar divide-and-rule tactics employed in Buganda. One local politician observed that, "Museveni is solely responsible for this mess. He antagonized the Bakonzo and Bamba by creating rival kingdoms… it was a setup."[37]

Matters worsened in 2016 when opposition candidate Dr. Kizza Besigye visited the region during his campaign and was warmly received by King Mumbere. The king publicly advised Museveni to retire and tend to his cattle—an unusually bold rebuke from a traditional leader. Stung by the public humiliation and a devastating electoral loss in Kasese District—where the ruling NRM lost all parliamentary and local council seats—President Museveni perceived the kingdom's alignment with the opposition as treachery.[38]

Although the precise trigger of the 2016 post-election violence in the Rwenzori region remains contested, multiple eyewitness accounts indicate that the unrest began when residents poured into the streets to celebrate the NRM's electoral defeat in this region. Security forces responded with lethal force, killing at least six people and injuring dozens more. Then-Inspector General of Police, Gen. Kale Kayihura, accused the Rwenzururu Kingdom of harboring a militia allegedly responsible for attacking police installations.[39] Kingdom officials, however, refuted these claims, asserting that security forces had targeted unarmed civilians engaged in peaceful celebration.[40] The situation further deteriorated when President Museveni ordered King Mumbere to disband his royal guards and accept protection from state security agencies. The king refused, emphasizing that the royal guards—traditionally armed with ceremonial spears and bows—were a culturally significant component of the monarchy and essential to its identity.

A violent standoff followed. A joint force of the UPDF and police stormed the king's palace using gunfire and rocket-propelled grenades, reducing it to ashes and killing over 180 people.[41] The government admitted to 87 deaths, but human rights organizations and medical responders put the toll far higher. The Red Cross reported at least 55 deaths on the first day and over 100 the next, including 15 children.[42]

The government claimed those killed were members of a secessionist "royal militia" allegedly pushing for a breakaway Yiira Republic. Yet no credible evidence substantiates this claim, and local voices have dismissed the Yiira Republic as state propaganda. One local observer states that "there is no such thing as the Yiira Republic—it's a fiction created by the government to justify its actions."[43] Human Rights Watch and other observers reported that the palace regularly hosted hundreds of civilians, including children, women, and youth engaged in vocational training and household tasks. Most of those killed, photographic evidence suggests, were unarmed.[44]

Museveni later gloated that King Mumbere had "reaped what he sowed," boasting that he had subdued the king without using the full might of the military.[45] His remarks revealed a disturbing disregard for civilian life.Local MPs accused the President of treating mass civilian deaths as acceptable collateral damage in his quest for power consolidation.[46] Citing a Luganda proverb, Museveni likened the king's action to crossing a river in a clay canoe—suggesting the disastrous outcome was self-inflicted.[47] Subsequently, the king was arrested and charged with murder, treason, and terrorism. Although he was later granted bail, he remains under de facto house arrest in the capital, Kampala, cut off from his kingdom for several years. No security officials have been held accountable for the loss of lives during the attack. Instead, Brig. Peter Elwelu, who led the operation, was promoted to Major General and named UPDF Land Forces Commander. The military spokesperson publicly declared that no investigation would be conducted.

The Rwenzururu crisis offers critical insight into how Museveni's regime confronts dissent from entrenched social structures. As with the 2009 Buganda protests, the military functions as the regime's primary instrument of coercion, routinely deployed to discipline constituencies perceived as defiant or disloyal. The army's loyalty is sustained through the strategic placement of trusted officers into key command positions. These individuals often view the regime as the fruit of their revolutionary struggle and, by extension, as their political inheritance. As one opposition MP explains, "Whenever we challenge the regime's coercive actions, the response is always: 'Where were you when we were fighting to liberate this country?'—implying that we have no moral authority to question their repression."[48] Reflecting on the events in Kasese, the MP concluded: "What happened there was the UPDF at its worst—they bombed the palace, massacred civilians, and buried the dead in military barracks to cover their tracks."[49]

Nationwide, military lockdowns followed the 2016 elections. Opposition leaders, including Besigye, Erias Lukwago, Ibrahim Ssemujju Nganda, Ingrid Turinawe, and Wafula Oguttu, were detained or placed under house arrest. Others, such as MP Michael Kabaziguruka, were jailed incommunicado and later charged with treason in military court despite being civilians. MP Kabaziguruka reflected: "How can you claim victory in a free election when you deploy the military everywhere to silence dissent? They accused me of plotting a mutiny—an absurd charge."[50]

Such patterns illustrate how Museveni has transformed the security apparatus into a political instrument. Promotions are reserved for loyalists willing to employ violence on the regime's behalf. The court martial, once a disciplinary tool for soldiers, now targets dissident voices—including civilians critical of the regime. Thus, the regime's strategy is clear: reward loyalty, punish defiance, and keep potential critics—military or civilian—under constant threat. Even in retirement, many former officials maintain silence, fearing the state holds incriminating material to be used should they challenge the status quo. The events in Kasese thus exemplify how the Museveni regime suppress dissent and reinforce its authoritarian grip.

Managing internal Dissent & Rewarding Loyal Cadres

While the military has played a central role in Uganda's post-conflict state reconstruction—particularly in reinforcing the ruling regime and key state institutions—it has also, alongside the police and intelligence agencies, assumed a dominant role in suppressing dissent within the regime itself. Powerful politicians and senior army officers who have expressed critical views of the regime have frequently faced arrest, detention, or prosecution on politically fabricated charges.

In response to mounting dissent within the ruling establishment, President Museveni has primarily relied on four strategies to neutralize internal critics. First, senior regime officials who publicly criticize the president are often dismissed from their positions or placed on forced leave—only to be politically rehabilitated later, typically after issuing a public apology or reaffirming their loyalty to the president. Second, in the case of dissenting military officers, Museveni has frequently employed informal mechanisms such as *katebe* (non-deployment), a form of internal exile within the army. Given the relatively modest official salaries in the military, prolonged periods of non-deployment are seen as punitive, as they deny officers access to the lucrative allowances associated with deployments and operational command.

Third, the regime deploys formal legal mechanisms—both through civilian courts and the military court martial—to prosecute critical voices within the security sector. In cases where the regime lacks confidence in securing a conviction, it often resorts to procedural tactics such as the deliberate delay of trials to frustrate and demoralize the accused. Finally, Museveni frequently engages in behind-the-scenes negotiations with officers who have fallen out of favor. He has consistently demonstrated a willingness to forgive those who "repent" and seek his pardon, thereby reinforcing his image as both a disciplinarian and a benevolent patriarch within the regime.

The public fallout between President Museveni and powerful army officers such as Maj. Gen. James Kazini, Lt. Gen. Henry Tumukunde, and Gen. David Sejusa underscores the extent to which Museveni perceives internal dissent as a serious threat to regime durability. These were highly respected figures who had played pivotal roles in the NRA's military campaign—serving as battle-hardened commanders and trusted allies of the president. Having been instrumental in Museveni's rise to power, they later became disillusioned with the direction the country was taking under his rule. As their concerns grew, they began to voice them publicly, issuing statements critical of Museveni and the NRM's leadership, thereby challenging the internal cohesion and ideological unity of the ruling establishment. In each case, Museveni followed a familiar script to neutralize dissent: arrest, detention, prosecution—often on questionable charges—and the deliberate delay of legal proceedings to prolong uncertainty and punishment without conviction.

In all three cases, the regime's objective was not to deliver swift justice, but to contain dissent—weaponizing legal and disciplinary mechanisms to enforce political loyalty and signal the high cost of defiance among the military elites. A striking example is Gen. David Sejusa, a former senior presidential advisor and coordinator of intelligence services, who was among the most influential commanders in the UPDF. A battle-hardened veteran of the NRA war, Sejusa held senior positions in the military and was a key member of the UPDF High Command—the army's supreme decision-making body. His rupture with Museveni became publicly evident in 1996, when he shocked the military establishment by testifying before a parliamentary committee and sharply criticizing the regime's handling of the LRA insurgency in northern Uganda. At the time, Sejusa was the overall commander of the counterinsurgency campaign against the LRA, and his public criticism deeply rattled both the regime and the military hierarchy. He was swiftly summoned to appear before the High Command for a dressing-down. However, before facing the reprimand, Sejusa pre-emptively submitted a resignation letter to Museveni—an unexpected and bold gesture that highlighted the seriousness of his disillusionment and set the stage for his gradual marginalization within the security establishment. In his letter, he noted that; "I find it unjustified to continue serving in an institution whose bodies I have no faith in or whose views I do not subscribe to…".[51]

President Museveni's refusal to grant General David Sejusa's retirement in 1996 marked the beginning of a long-running standoff between a powerful regime insider and the state he once served. While Museveni cited unspecified "problems" as the reason for denying retirement,[52] analysts speculated that the real motive was to neutralize Sejusa's perceived political ambitions.[53] As a decorated founding member of the NRA, Sejusa posed a unique threat—his popularity in the military and record in the bush war made him a potential political rival. The regime adopted a strategic approach to contain him by using legal and bureaucratic mechanisms to block his exit from the army, leveraging a constitutional clause that bars serving officers from participating in politics.[54]

When Sejusa sought legal redress, the Constitutional Court ruled in his favor. However, the Supreme Court—widely viewed as politically compromised—overturned this decision on procedural grounds.[55] The regime effectively immobilized Sejusa by placing him on *Katebe* (non-deployment) for over a decade. In 2004, Sejusa publicly apologized to Museveni and was reinstated as Coordinator of National Intelligence.[56] This move, however, tethered him even more closely to regime operations, and he was later linked to repressive actions, including the 2005 arrest of Besigye and the 2010 crackdown on media during the Buganda protests.

In 2013, Sejusa reignited national debate by releasing a letter alleging an assassination plot targeting high-profile officials opposed to the so-called "Muhoozi Project"—a purported plan to install Museveni's son as successor.[57] He named senior security officers as conspirators and accused the regime of framing and eliminating dissenters.[58] His claims were explosive not only because they came from within the intelligence apparatus, but because they exposed internal fissures in the military over succession politics.[59] The mysterious death of Gen. Aronda Nyakairima shortly, thereafter, coupled with the government's opaque response, fueled public suspicion.[60] In an effort to suppress the fallout, the state shut down media houses that published Sejusa's letter, prompting the general to flee to exile in London.

From his exile in London, Sejusa made further allegations, including involvement in rigging the 2006 elections, claiming Museveni had received just 30% of the vote.[61] He also spoke on the suspicious death of MP Cerinah Nebanda in 2012, which triggered a major standoff between parliament and the executive.[62] Although the state claimed she died of a drug overdose, MPs and her family alleged foul play, pointing to her outspoken criticism of regime corruption and her opposition to the oil bill. Attempts by parliament to investigate her death were met with arrests, media intimidation, and even threats against the Speaker of Parliament.[63] Sejusa later claimed insider knowledge of how Nebanda's death was orchestrated by regime insiders angered by her defiance. He alleged—without providing concrete evidence—that a meeting involving Museveni, his wife, son, and other relatives approved measures to eliminate dissenters within the ruling party.[64] These revelations triggered new waves of speculation about the first family's grip on power and the use of state violence to suppress internal dissent. In 2014, Sejusa unexpectedly returned to Uganda, was received with military honors, and shiftily driven from the airport to a meeting with President Museveni, further signaling a behind-the-scenes reconciliation.

Despite presidential assurances, Sejusa's name was omitted from the official army retirement list, prompting him to petition the High Court, which ruled he had been constructively discharged due to prolonged non-deployment and the withdrawal of benefits. Although the army appealed the ruling, the case remained unresolved until 2022 when, following secretive negotiations with the President, Sejusa was formally retired at a ceremony presided over by Museveni.[65] Since then, he has remained politically inactive, living in seclusion in the countryside—widely interpreted by observers as a condition imposed by the regime in exchange for his retirement.

The Sejusa saga underscores the regime's dilemma in managing elite dissent, especially among powerful army officers. Museveni's options—repression through court martial or prolonged administrative detention—have both proven destabilizing. Trials of prominent generals, such as Tumukunde in 2005, have backfired, with civil courts often overturning the military court's rulings and exposing intra-elite tensions. These developments reveal that while Museveni retains dominance, his authority faces intermittent pushback from within the very institutions that sustain his rule.

Museveni has employed a similar containment strategy against other dissenting military elites, notably Lt. Gen. Henry Tumukunde. In 2005, Tumukunde—then head of the Internal Security Organisation (ISO)—was dismissed from his post and lost his parliamentary seat after publicly opposing the removal of presidential term limits. He was subsequently placed under house arrest for two years and prosecuted by the court martial, a legal process that stretched over eight years. Although initially charged with serious offenses, including spreading harmful propaganda, the court ultimately convicted him of the lesser charge of conduct prejudicial to military discipline and issued only a formal warning.[66] Tumukunde successfully challenged his dismissal in the Supreme Court, which ruled it unlawful. Despite his legal victory, his request for retirement was denied for several years. Eventually, in what was widely perceived as a product of behind-the-scenes negotiations, Tumukunde was promoted directly to the rank of Lieutenant General—skipping the rank of Major General—in a gesture interpreted as a political reconciliation with President Museveni. Less than a month after his promotion, he was formally retired from the army.[67] He later contested the 2021 presidential election as an independent but was unsuccessful. Following the election, Tumukunde appeared to re-align with the regime and has since been rehabilitated, competing as the ruling party's flagbearer in the race for a parliamentary seat ahead of the 2026 elections.

Another illuminating case is that of General James Kazini, a former army commander and once one of Museveni's most loyal military allies. Despite playing a pivotal role in consolidating NRM's military dominance in the late 1990s and early 2000s, Kazini eventually fell out of favor. In 2003, he was dismissed and sent on a military course in Nigeria after being implicated—alongside several other officers—in a scandal involving ghost soldiers and mismanagement of military logistics.[68] Tensions escalated when Kazini publicly contradicted Museveni, claiming the President had long been aware of the ghost soldier scheme.[69] This unprecedented defiance sparked media speculation and led to Kazini's recall and arraignment before a court martial. He and 28 officers were accused of fraudulently inserting 440 phantom names into the payroll of the army's 507 Brigade and misappropriating funds.[70]

However, Kazini's prosecution occurred only after he became openly critical of the regime. Other implicated officers, such as Henry Tumukunde, Nakibus Lakara, Julius Oketta, John Mugume, Fred Tolit, and Andrew Gutti, maintained loyalty and were ultimately rewarded with promotions and reinstatements. Their silence stood in contrast to Kazini's defiance. Although they were initially suspended alongside him, the charges against them were quietly dropped—underscoring the regime's selective use of corruption allegations to punish disloyalty while shielding compliant loyalists. In Kazini's case, additional charges were brought for disobeying lawful orders and unauthorized troop movements—offenses that carry severe penalties under military law. He denied all charges and sought redress in the Constitutional Court, which temporarily suspended the court martial proceedings.[71]

Kazini's case illustrates how corruption is weaponized within the military to enforce loyalty and punish dissent.[72] Officers who challenge Museveni risk court martial, dismissal, or worse. Before the court could deliver a final ruling, Kazini died under mysterious circumstances in November 2009. While the state claimed he was killed in a domestic altercation, family members and political observers suspect he was assassinated, citing his claim that funds tied to the ghost soldiers' scandal had been sanctioned to pay Congolese rebel leaders.[73] His death was widely perceived as politically motivated.[74] Museveni's cryptic remark at Kazini's funeral—that the general had "taken himself to God"—only deepened public suspicion and underscored the peril faced by military elites who fall out with the President.[75]

The cases of Generals Sejusa, Tumukunde, and Kazini reveal a consistent pattern in Museveni's management of internal dissent within the military—i.e., combining coercion, co-optation, and selective enforcement of legal and institutional mechanisms. Officers who challenge the President's authority, question succession plans, or expose regime misconduct are met with harsh reprisals, including surveillance, court martial, prolonged detention, and public vilification. Yet, as seen in the cases of Sejusa and Tumukunde, the regime also leaves space for strategic reconciliation, often through opaque negotiations that restore privileges in exchange for political silence or rehabilitation. In contrast, Kazini's fate illustrates the regime's zero-tolerance approach to defiant officers who persist in exposing internal contradictions. Museveni's control over disciplinary institutions like the court martial, his use of military promotions as political rewards, and his politicisation of corruption charges underscore a broader logic of authoritarian survival—one that secures elite loyalty through a mix of intimidation and patronage, while sending a clear message that dissent within the political and security establishment carries profound personal risk.

Notes

1. Karugire S.R. (1988) ibid. 94.
2. Kiranda Y and Kamp M. (2010) "The State of Multi-party Democracy in Uganda" ***Konrad Adnauer Stiftung***. Available online: http://www.kas.de/wf/doc/kas_21611-1522-2-30.pdf?110113145556.
3. Gloppen, S., Kasimbazi, E. & Kibandama, A. (2006) 'The Evolving Role of the Courts in the Political Transition Process', (CHR Michelsen Institute, Makerere University, Uganda).
4. Akaki S. (2007) "Is the People's Redemption Army a Benevolent Rebel Group?" October 20th. All Africa.com. Available online: https://allafrica.com/stories/200710220548.html.
5. CNN (2005) "Treason Case pressed at Summit" November 25. Available online: http://www.cnn.com/2005/world/africa/11/25/uganda.treason/= ..
6. BBC (2007) Available "Uganda's judges strike over raid" March 5. online: http://news.bbc.co.uk/2/hi/africa/6418943.stm.
7. Ellett R.L. (2008) "Emerging Judicial Power in Transitional Democracies: Malawi, Tanzania and Uganda" PhD dissertation, PhD dissertation, Northeastern University Boston, Ma. Available online: https://repository.library.northeastern.edu/files/neu:1885/fulltext.pdf.
8. New Vision (2010) "Col. Besigye Treason Case Dismissed." October 12. Available online: https://www.newvision.co.ug/new_vision/news/1280940/col-besigye-treason-dismissed.

9. The Guardian (2006) "Uganda's Chief Opposition Leader Cleared of Rape" March 8. Available online: https://www.theguardian.com/world/2006/mar/08/uganda.mainsection.
10. Justice John Bosco Katutsi's ruling is available online: The judgment is available at www.judicature.go.ug/uploaded_ les/1142236737Besigye-rape%20case-Judgement.pdf.
11. Interview with Francis Mwijukye.ibid.
12. Chimpreports (2015) "Inside Maj Rabwoni Arrest at Entebbe Airport" June 8. Available online: http://www.chimpreports.com/inside-maj-rabwoni-arrest-at-entebbe-airport/.
13. Chimp reports .2015June 8. Ibid.
14. Kobusigye O. (2010) *The Correct Line? Uganda Under Museveni* Author House, UK.
15. New Vision, May 27, 2002.
16. Daily Monitor (2006) "Three Killed at Besigye's Meet" February 16. Available online: http://allafrica.com/stories/200602150824.html.
17. Olive Kobusingye, Ibid, pg 34.
18. The UPDF Act 2005.
19. Bareebe G. and Titeca K. (2013) "Personalization of Power under the Museveni Regime in Uganda" L'Afrique des Grands Lacs, Annuaire, Paris, France.
20. Byenkya, A., (2011) "
Kampala: New Vision, Feb. 5, 2011, Army to work with police to quell poll violence – Muhoozi.
21. Interview with Ladislaus Rwakafuzi.ibid.
22. Interview with Ingrid Turinawe, one of the organizers of the walk-to-work protests (September 4, 2016).
23. Daily Monitor (2013) "Museveni tells MPs: Army can Take over." January 18. Available online: http://www.monitor.co.ug/News/National/Museveni-tells-MPs--Army-can-take-over/688334-1668782-i1kjtj/index.html.
24. Daily monitor (2013) "Aronda says Army Takeover is possible" January 24. Available online: http://www.monitor.co.ug/News/National/Aronda-says-army-takeover-possible/688334-1673856-11mfejrz/index.html.

25. Daily Monitor (2013) "Don't tempt the Army-Kiyongo." January 20. Available: http://www.monitor.co.ug/News/National/Don-t-tempt-the-army---Kiyonga/688334-1669654-14jonv/index.html Also see: "Museveni tells MPs: Army can Takeover" (January 18, 2013) Available online: http://www.monitor.co.ug/News/National/Museveni-tells-MPs--Army-can-take-over/688334-1668782-i1kjtj/index.html.
26. Onyango-Obbo C. (2013) "Military coup? In Uganda? That's a tautology, surely." The East African (January 26) Available online: http://www.theeastafrican.co.ke/OpEd/comment/Military-coup-In-Uganda-That-is-a-tautology/434750-1675782-k86ihe/index.html.
27. Kayunga, S. S. (2000) "The Federo (federalism) debate in Uganda" (Working Paper No. 62) Kampala: Centre for Basic Research. p. 28.
28. International Crisis Group report (2012) "No resolution to growing crisis" Brussels: African Report No. 187.
29. Interview with Hon. Muwanga Kivumbi, Ibid.
30. Human Rights Watch, (2010) "World Report 2010: Uganda", Published by Human rights watch, available online www.hrw.org/world-report-2011/Uganda.
31. Human Rights Watch, (2010) "World Report 2010: Uganda", Published by Human rights watch, available online www.hrw.org/world-report-2011/Uganda.
32. Golooba-Mutebi F. (2011) ibid. P.10–25.
33. Human Rights Watch 2010 report.
34. Human Rights Watch. Ibid.
35. Interview with Hon. Muwanga Kivumbi.ibid.
36. Shahuka-Muhundo A. and Titeca K. (2016) "The Rwenzururu Movement and the Struggle for the Rwenzururu Kingdom in Uganda" IOB *discussion paper* / 2016. 2294–86.
37. See, for example, an Interview of Winfred Kizza, area woman member of parliament in the Daily Monitor, December 28, 2016) Available online: http://www.monitor.co.ug/News/National/MP-Kiiza-blames-clashes-on-govt--seeks-talks/688334-3467954-iu76epz/index.html.
38. Interview with Hon. Francis Mwijukye, ibid.

39. New Vision (2016) "Why Besigye Beats Museveni in Kasese" March 27.Available online: http://www.newvision.co.ug/new_vision/news/1151719/besigye-beats-museveni-kasese.
40. Uganda Radio Network (2016) "Kasese Attacks Fueled by Rwenzururu Kingdom Militia – Kayihura" March 13. Available online: https://ugandaradionetwork.com/story/kale-kayihura-militias-who-attacked-security-personnel-are-linked-to-obusinga-wa-rwenzururu.
41. Daily Monitor (2016) "Museveni Defends attack on Rwenzuru Palace" December 7. Available online: http://www.monitor.co.ug/News/National/Museveni-defends-attack-on-Rwenzururu-palace/688334-3478456-hmtpno/index.html.
42. Report by the Human Rights Watch, March 2017.
43. Interview with Asuman Bisiika. Ibid.
44. Report by the Human Rights Watch, March 2017.
45. See Museveni's Statement on Kasese and Bundibugyo attacks. Available online: http://www.newvision.co.ug/new_vision/news/1342421/museveni-speaks-kasese-bundibugyo-attacks.
46. See the Interview of Winfred Kizza, area woman member of parliament in Daily Monitor (December 28, 2016) Available online: http://www.monitor.co.ug/News/National/MP-Kiiza-blames-clashes-on-govt--seeks-talks/688334-3467954-iu76epz/index.html.
47. See Museveni's Statement on Kasese and Bundibugyo attacks. Available online: http://www.newvision.co.ug/new_vision/news/1342421/museveni-speaks-kasese-bundibugyo-attacks.
48. Interview with Mwijukye Francis. Ibid.
49. Interview with Mwijukye Francis. Ibid.
50. Interview with Michael Kabaziguruka ibid.
51. Gen. David Sejusa's letter to Museveni. Available online: https://niyibizi.wordpress.com/2016/02/07/.
52. Interview with Felix Kulayigye.ibid.
53. Daily Monitor (2013) "Police Raid Tinyefunza's Office" May 12. Available online: http://www.monitor.co.ug/News/National/Military-police-raid-Gen--Tinyefuza-s-office/688334-1849240-view-printVersion-u6wd7rz/index.html.
54. Recently, Justice George Kanyeihamba, a retired member of the Uganda Supreme Court criticized his colleagues on the bench for changing their rulings after phone calls with the President in 2006

when they handled a petition challenging Museveni's electoral victory.

55. The Eagle online (2016) "Museveni vs Sejusa: the three-decade battle between Uganda's two most prominent Generals." May 30. Available online: http://eagle.co.ug/2016/05/30/museveni-vs-sejusa-three-decade-battle-ugandas-two-prominent-generals.html.
56. The Monitor (2016) "David Sejusa–the Daring General." February 7. Available online: http://allafrica.com/stories/201602081316.html.
57. Gen. Sejusa's Letter ibid.
58. Rhodes T. (2013) "In Uganda, media muzzled over alleged Muhoozi project" *Committee to Project Journalist*. Available online: https://cpj.org/blog/2013/05/in-uganda-media-muzzled-over-alleged-muhoozi-proje.php.
59. Sejusa's letter, ibid. pg26.
60. The East African (2015) "Nyakairima's death: Radio Katwe, Social Media Explode with Conspiracy Theories." September 19. Available online at: http://www.theeastafrican.co.ke/news/What-really-killed-Gen-Aronda-/-/2558/2876782/-/99w04v/-/index.html.
61. African Review (2013) "Exiled Ugandan General Says Museveni Stole 2006 Elections" December 17. (Available online: http://www.africareview.com/news/Exiled-Uganda-general-says-Museveni-stole-election/979180-2115434-10ah9y9/index.html
62. See, for example an Interview with Hon. Chris Baryomunsi, a Member of Parliament for Kinkizi East, as published by NRW media. The transcript of this interview is available online at https://www.rnw.org/archive/what-or-who-killed-ugandan-mp-cerinah-nebanda.
63. Esptein H. (2016) Ibid.
64. Esptein H. (2016) Ibid.
65. New Vision (2015) "Museveni Meets gen. Sejusa" (January 3) Available online: http://www.newvision.co.ug/new_vision/news/1318440/president-museveni-meets-gen-sejusa.
66. Daily Monitor (2013) "Brig. Tumukunde Sentenced to Serious Warning" April 18. Available online at http://www.monitor.co.ug/News/National/Brig--Tumukunde-sentenced-to-serious-warning/688334-1751938-j0hmlwz/index.html.

67. Daily Monitor (2015) "Tumukunde Promoted, then Retired." September 1. (Available online at http://www.monitor.co.ug/News/National/Brig-Tumukunde-promoted--then-retired/688334-2854028-k7slfyz/index.html.
68. New Vision (2003) "Kazini to Face Court Martial" December 1. Available online: http://www.newvision.co.ug/new_vision/news/1254989/kazini-court-martial.
69. Kobusingye, O. (2010), Ibid.
70. Atuhaire, B. A. (2005) "Paymaster in Trouble for Exposing Ghost Soldiers" The Monitor, August 12. Available online: http://allafrica.com/stories/200508110955.html.
71. *Afedraru*, L. (2009) "*Judge saves Kazini from court martial*", The Monitor, April 16.
72. Kibirige, D. (2001) "UPDF Officer Tries to Kill Congo Paymaster Ghosts On Payroll" The Monitor (2001) "UPDF Officer Tries to Kill Congo Paymaster Ghosts On Payroll" May 5. (Available online: http://allafrica.com/stories/200105070054.html
73. Mwenda, M. A. (2009) "Who killed Gen. Kazini, and why?" *The Independent Magazine*, November 24. Available online: https://www.independent.co.ug/killed-gen-kazini/.
74. Wanabwa R. (2013) "Kazini Family Wants Fresh Death Probe" The Monitor, November 10. Available online: http://www.monitor.co.ug/News/National/Kazini-family-wants-fresh-death-probe/688334-2067046-kndqoyz/index.html.
75. Mwenda, A. (2009). Ibid.

CHAPTER 7

Outsourcing Repression: Vigilantes and Third-Party Violence Under the NRM

Situating Non-State Violent Actors in post-1986 Ugandan Politics

Scholars of political science have long examined the relationship between authoritarian regimes and non-state violent actors.[1] The prevailing literature suggests that vigilante violence is often symptomatic of state weakness and a perceived lack of legitimacy in the eyes of the public.[2] Some scholars argue that regimes deliberately deploy or tolerate vigilante groups as instruments of intimidation and coercion, using them to suppress dissent and reinforce political control.[3] Others focus on the broader implications of vigilante activity for the state's monopoly on the use of force, noting how such violence undermines formal authority and blurs the boundaries between legitimate and illegitimate coercion.[4] A parallel strand of research contends that civilians may resort to vigilante or self-help violence when they view the state as unwilling, unable, or untrustworthy in its duty to provide security.[5] In Kenya, for instance, studies have documented the rise of vigilante groups deeply embedded within political and local patronage networks, effectively replacing or co-opting the functions of state security agencies.[6] Similarly, in Nigeria, groups such as the Bush Boys, Ateke Tom's Niger Delta Vigilantes, and the Greenlanders were often deployed by previous military regimes to suppress opposition and consolidate power.[7]

G. Bareebe, *Social Structures and the Making of Museveni's Civil-Authoritarian Regime in Uganda*,
https://doi.org/10.1007/978-3-032-14015-9_7

Existing literature on Museveni's regime tend to overlook the direct role of the state in organizing and deploying vigilante groups to supply violence. Yet the NRM strategically employs vigilante groups as covert extensions of its coercive apparatus—an informal, deniable mechanism for enforcing authority and ensuring regime durability. Far from being a symptom of state weakness, the use of vigilante violence in Uganda is a deliberate strategy for maintaining political control. The NRM views vigilantes as essential to regime survival and deploys them systematically to suppress opposition mobilization, enforce compliance with unpopular policies, and intimidate segments of the population. By outsourcing repression to these non-state actors, the Museveni deflects blame and obscures its own accountability for the violence perpetrated against unarmed civilians and political opponents. In this context, vigilante groups function not only as instruments of coercion but also as political cover, enabling the state to obscure its violent character behind a façade of community-based security.

Following the NRM ascent to power in 1986, Uganda did not experience organized vigilante violence until the 2001 presidential election, when President Yoweri Museveni faced a formidable challenger, Dr. Kizza Besigye. A former comrade-in-arms of Museveni during the "bush war" that brought the NRA to power, Besigye's decision to contest the presidency was both unexpected and politically consequential. Despite Uganda being a de facto one-party state at the time, Besigye challenged Museveni's authority, leveraging his own popularity, military credentials, and reformist image. Dr. Besigye had served as a military doctor during the civil war, treating numerous high-ranking NRA fighters, which earned him significant respect within the army and the ruling elite. He rose rapidly through the ranks to become a colonel and held key positions, including Commander of the NRA's mechanized brigade and Minister of Internal Affairs by the age of 29. As the NRM's National Political Commissar, Besigye played a pivotal role in building the party's local council structures from the village to the district level. While relatively unknown to the broader Ugandan public at the time, his stature within the regime and military circles was notable. However, his meteoric rise and growing political ambition began to unsettle the regime's leadership. By the late 1990s, Museveni began reassigning Besigye to peripheral roles—widely interpreted as an effort to curtail his influence and popularity.

Besigye's decision to contest Museveni's rule, though surprising to many external observers, had long been anticipated by insiders familiar with his political acumen and grassroots mobilization capacity. His work as Political Commissar had provided him with valuable networks and visibility within NRM.[8] Upon launching his presidential campaign, Besigye embarked on a nationwide tour, sharply criticizing Museveni for deviating from the NRA's original ten-point program. He accused the president of failing to democratize the government, curb corruption, and uphold the ideals for which the NRA had fought. His bold rhetoric, military background, and charisma attracted widespread support, drawing thousands to his rallies and energizing a disillusioned electorate.[9]

Besigye's growing popularity also fractured the ruling coalition. Several moderate NRM members who had grown critical of Museveni's leadership defected to Besigye's camp, shaking the political establishment. As his challenge to the regime gained momentum, informal regime-aligned vigilante groups began to emerge, playing a significant role in suppressing votes and intimidating Besigye's supporters. These actors—operating in the gray zones between state and non-state violence—signaled a shift in the NRM's coercive strategies, marking the resurgence of organized vigilante violence as a tool for political control in Uganda's evolving authoritarian landscape.[10] In what follows, I trace the emergence, structure, and operations of key vigilante groups in Uganda, illustrating how their integration into the NRM's governance strategy reinforces regime durability and authoritarian resilience.

The Kalangala Action Plan (KAP)

During the 2001 and 2006 general elections, a particularly notorious vigilante outfit—the Kalangala Action Plan (KAP)—emerged in Kampala. Unlike the Crime Preventers and the Kiboko Squad, which were largely composed of civilians, KAP was comprised of active-duty soldiers, often seen brandishing AK-47 rifles. The group quickly gained notoriety for its violent repression of Ugandans opposed to President Museveni's re-election. Reports of torture, enforced disappearances, and extrajudicial killings circulated widely, and some opposition figures and activists were allegedly abducted and detained by KAP operatives.

The existence of the KAP was a closely guarded secret until 2001, when local media outlets published video clips and photographs showing its members undergoing military training in the wilderness of Luwero

District.[11] These revelations came just before the group was deployed on the streets of Kampala to suppress opposition mobilization activities. KAP operated under the command of Major Roland Kakooza Mutale, who was then serving as a presidential advisor for special duties. The group was particularly active in Uganda's central and northern regions, where President Museveni faced strong electoral competition.[12] Initially, the government denied knowledge of the group's activities, with both the police and army issuing statements disavowing any formal links to KAP, despite mounting evidence of its operations and close coordination with state security forces.

Human rights organizations and the media publicly condemned KAP for acts of torture and enforced disappearance, yet no member of the group was ever arrested or prosecuted. Its commander, Major Kakooza Mutale, a former NRA rebel officer and one of President Museveni's most loyal allies, regularly appeared in local media to justify KAP's actions. In his statements, Mutale openly defended the group's use of force and affirmed that President Museveni was both aware of and supportive of KAP's mission to target political opponents.[13]

KAP vigilantes became infamous for their violent tactics—assaulting, detaining, and intimidating opposition activists with complete impunity. Armed with firearms, they routinely abducted and tortured individuals in clandestine detention facilities known as "safe houses," where detainees were held incommunicado and subjected to severe abuse.[14]

Reports of KAP's brutality shocked the nation when victims appeared in the media bearing fresh wounds and visible signs of torture. Survivors recounted harrowing experiences of physical and psychological abuse, often aimed at extracting information about planned opposition mobilization efforts. The Uganda Human Rights Commission (UHRC) received over 7,500 complaints related to KAP's operations. These revelations sparked widespread condemnation from politicians, church leaders, civil society organizations, and traditional authorities, who accused KAP and Major Mutale of using torture to persecute political dissenters.

Despite mounting evidence, the government denied any association with KAP. The Minister of Internal Affairs, as well as the heads of the police and national intelligence services, publicly claimed that the group did not exist. In response to public outcry, a parliamentary committee was established to investigate the violence that had marred the 2001 elections. Major Mutale was summoned to testify before the committee. In a widely publicized and theatrical display, he arrived at Parliament under full military escort, accompanied by a brass band and two busloads of supporters dressed in NRM party colors. Addressing the Members of Parliament, Mutale defended KAP as a voluntary organization with two primary objectives: first, to mobilize support for President Museveni and the ruling party; and second, to crush what he described as "undisciplined individuals who stood against our Chairman, Yoweri Museveni."[15]

Following the conclusion of the 2001 general elections, the KAP continued its operations, with a sustained focus on targeting opposition figures and activists associated with the Reform Agenda—a political pressure group formed by Dr. Besigye, which later evolved into the main opposition party, the Forum for Democratic Change (FDC). By 2005, several high-ranking NRM leaders and former military officers had fallen out with President Museveni and joined the opposition. Many of these ex-army officers garnered significant support from disillusioned youth, who were increasingly frustrated with NRM rule in Uganda.[16]

KAP publicly justified its continued operations as necessary to contain what it described as radicalized youth "hell-bent on causing violence and internal instability" in Uganda.[17] Between 2001 and 2006, KAP actively recruited and indoctrinated thousands of young people in its camps located in Luwero District. On average, approximately 600 youth were brought to these camps each month, where they underwent military drills, basic training in military science, and civic education. KAP leaders frequently appeared in the media defending their activities and asserting the importance of their mission.

The peak of KAP's brutal operations occurred during the 2006 and 2011 general elections, when the group became heavily involved in coercive and clandestine efforts aimed at suppressing emerging anti-NRM social and political movements. In a notable media interview, Maj. Kakooza Mutale stated that KAP's primary objective was to dismantle the mobilization efforts of former military officers who had defected from the NRM to join the opposition—specifically naming Generals Mugisha Muntu, David Tinyefuza (also known as Sejusa), and Colonel Kizza Besigye.[18] According to Mutale, had KAP not intervened, the Museveni regime could have been overthrown by these ex-military leaders by 2016. The source of funding for KAP's operations remained a closely guarded secret. However, several Members of Parliament sitting on the Parliamentary Committee for Defence and Internal Affairs suggested that KAP was covertly financed through UPDF's classified security budget.[19]

The Kiboko Squad

The Kiboko Squad first emerged in 2007 when it violently dispersed peaceful demonstrators who were protesting the government's proposal to allocate part of Mabira Forest, a national forest reserve, to a sugarcane corporation. During the protest, members of the Kiboko Squad appeared alongside anti-riot police, armed with clubs and sticks, and aggressively beat civilians. The group quickly gained notoriety for its brutality, particularly during the 2011 post-election protests, where it was implicated in widespread assaults on opposition supporters and bystanders.

Unlike the Kalangala Action Plan (KAP), which operated under a clearly defined command structure, the leadership of the Kiboko Squad remained obscure. A man named Juma Semakula, popularly known as 'Backfire', appeared publicly claiming to lead the group, though his actual authority and affiliations were unclear. Many political observers and human rights activists suspected that the squad was created and directed by the then Inspector General of Police, General Kale Kayihura. These suspicions were fueled by the fact that the squad's operational base appeared to be the Kampala Central Police Station (CPS).[20]

Further evidence suggested deep collusion between the police and the vigilante group. Reports revealed that the clubs and iron bars used by Kiboko Squad members were transported into the city using police pick-up trucks stationed at CPS. Although the police spokesperson publicly denied any involvement by the police leadership in forming or coordinating the group, she failed to explain several inconsistencies—such as why police vehicles were seen transporting vigilantes across Kampala, or why the police catering department was providing them with meals during their deployment. Additionally, the police consistently refrained from arresting or stopping Kiboko Squad members, even as they assaulted civilians in full view of law enforcement officers, raising serious concerns about state complicity.[21]

Despite sustained local and international criticism regarding the growing role of vigilante groups in Ugandan politics, the Kiboko Squad continued to operate, primarily targeting opposition groups and human rights activists throughout 2010 to 2017. One particularly alarming incident occurred on June 9, 2010, at the Clock Tower in Kampala, sending shockwaves across the nation. On that day, a group of opposition supporters staged a peaceful demonstration demanding electoral reforms.[22] Without warning, a swarm of Kiboko Squad vigilantes—armed with sticks and metal bars—descended on the protestors, severely beating and injuring many. Although there was a heavy deployment of both military and police personnel at the scene, the security forces did not intervene. Instead, they passively observed—some in visible disbelief—as the ununiformed assailants brutalized civilians. The vigilantes appeared highly coordinated, disciplined, and shielded by the presence of the armed forces.

Following the Clock Tower incident, media investigations suggested that the Kiboko Squad was not merely an ad hoc group of concerned citizens but was instead organized, equipped, and commanded by senior figures within Uganda's security establishment.[23] As public outrage and parliamentary pressure mounted in response to the attack, President Museveni eventually addressed the issue, though he stopped short of officially acknowledging state sponsorship of the group. In his remarks, Museveni stated that he was aware of and impressed by what he referred to as the "self-defense" actions of Ugandans who sought to protect themselves from opposition-led disruptions.[24] He described Kiboko Squad members as "good, patriotic citizens" defending themselves against "bad ones."[25] Museveni further revealed that, upon learning of the group's existence, he was initially concerned that it might consist of police officers. However, he claimed to have been reassured by intelligence services that the individuals involved were ordinary citizens who had voluntarily organized to resist rioters. He concluded by stating, "I salute these Ugandans who stood by justice and opposed criminals."[26]

This public endorsement—though veiled—served as a powerful signal of state complicity and implicit approval, further emboldening the Kiboko Squad and reinforcing a broader trend in which the Ugandan regime outsourced repression to non-state actors operating with near-total impunity.

In 2011, the National Electoral Commission (EC) was compelled to cancel the Kampala mayoral election due to widespread violence against voters perpetrated by Kiboko Squad vigilantes. In Rubaga Division, for instance, members of the group armed with sticks and nail-spiked clubs violently attacked voters in full view of police officers.[27] Eyewitnesses and media reports documented vigilantes arresting protesters, forcibly throwing them onto police pickup trucks, and transporting them to undisclosed detention facilities. Despite a heavy police deployment at the scene, law enforcement officers neither intervened to halt the abuses nor held the perpetrators accountable. Photographs published in the media showed Kiboko Squad vigilantes using police vehicles to arrest and detain civilians, prompting an unusually candid statement from the police spokesperson. She publicly criticized the officers involved and promised an internal investigation—yet the findings were never released, and no officer was ever held accountable, underscoring the entrenched culture of impunity.[28]

Shortly after the election violence, Juma Ssemakula, the alleged leader of the Kiboko Squad, appeared in the media and openly claimed to have commanded the vigilantes involved in the attacks. He asserted that he had coordinated with the police and other security agencies during the operation. Ssemakula's unauthorized public statements appeared to catch the state apparatus off guard. In response, the Inspector General of Police publicly rebuked Ssemakula, accusing him of tarnishing the image of the police.[29] When confronted by journalists with video evidence showing coordinated operations between vigilantes and uniformed officers—including shared use of police vehicles—Kayihura insisted that the Kiboko Squad was not affiliated with the police. He admitted that any officers collaborating with vigilantes were doing so without authorization and would face disciplinary action.

Following Ssemakula's media appearance, in which he boasted of assaulting civilians who opposed President Museveni, Gen. Kayihura ordered his arrest and prosecution. He also directed police detectives to investigate officers captured by the media assisting the Kiboko Squad in beating journalists and violently manhandling women and children during the electoral unrest. Ssemakula was arrested in March 2011 and detained at Kireka, a development that was welcomed by many Ugandans.[30] However, a segment of the public remained skeptical, questioning whether the arrest was merely a symbolic gesture intended to create the illusion that the government was serious about addressing the impunity of vigilante groups.

Public discourse, particularly on social media, reflected deep mistrust of the government's narrative. Many Ugandans expressed doubt that a relatively obscure individual like Ssemakula could have single-handedly orchestrated the extensive and coordinated violence attributed to the Kiboko Squad. These suspicions were seemingly validated when, just a few days after his arrest, Ssemakula was released without charge.[31] The police claimed that although Ssemakula had admitted involvement in the squad's actions, he had only participated "as an observer," not an active perpetrator.[32] According to police officials, this technicality rendered his prosecution legally untenable.[33] His release reinforced widespread concerns about state complicity, selective enforcement of the law, and the instrumentalization of vigilante violence in Ugandan electoral politics.

The Crime Preventors Program (CPP)

As Uganda was still reeling from the brutal legacy of the Kiboko Squad and the Kalangala Action Plan (KAP), a new youth vigilante force called crime preventers emerged in the lead-up to the 2016 election.[34] Unlike previous formations, CPP was openly developed and implemented by top figures in the security apparatus with the full approval of President Museveni. Police Chief Gen. Kale Kayihura was tasked with overseeing its rollout.[35] In contrast to KAP and the Kiboko Squad—whose ties to state institutions were often disguised—the CPP was officially sanctioned and backed by the police and military intelligence. The program involved training thousands of youths in martial arts and basic paramilitary tactics. The recruits, largely drawn from unemployed youth in villages, towns, universities, and tertiary institutions, were trained by police and army officers. The training sessions, held on school playgrounds and public spaces across all sub-counties, were conducted openly and were widely reported by media and civil society organizations. Participants were required to pledge allegiance to President Museveni and the ruling NRM party as a condition for joining. Officially, crime preventers were expected to patrol communities, report crimes, and support local law enforcement.

During the 2016 general elections, CPP members emerged as a key mobilization arm for the NRM. They canvassed villages and towns, urging residents to attend Museveni's campaign rallies—particularly in response to the popularity of opposition of Kizza Besigye, whose youthful support base posed an unprecedented challenge to the regime.[36] Museveni frequently attended CPP pass-out ceremonies as guest of honor, signaling his endorsement.[37] At these events, new recruits typically wore yellow NRM T-shirts emblazoned with Museveni's image. The police claimed that as many as 12 million Ugandans had been recruited into the program, though this figure was never independently verified.[38]

Unlike previous vigilante groups, the CPP had a formalized national structure, stretching from village-level coordinators to a National Secretariat based in Wandegeya, a Kampala suburb. The program was integrated into the state's formal structure, working closely with police units, intelligence officers, and Resident District Commissioners (RDCs)—the NRM's ideological custodians at the district level.[39] RDCs were tasked with supervising recruitment, screening applicants for their political beliefs, organizing seminars, and officiating graduations. One RDC justified the program as ideological re-education, stating that; "Many of our young people have forgotten what the NRM stands for... We are trying to teach them about where we have come from and the contribution of President Museveni to Uganda."[40]

Yet interviews with former crime preventers reveal a more complex reality. Many youths joined not out of ideological conviction but in the expectation of material rewards. Several recalled promises of employment or start-up capital. Moses Tumuhaise, a CPP recruit from Mbarara, recounted: "A recruitment officer told us we would be enlisted as police officers after the 2016 election if we performed well... But this was a lie. We were abandoned after the elections."[41]

Despite the program's mass appeal, it was plagued by poor oversight, indiscipline, and growing concerns—even within the regime—that such a large force of unemployed and trained youth could become a security threat. Civil society, religious institutions, monarchies, and the media raised alarms over CPP's activities. Reports emerged linking crime preventers to robberies, assault, extortion, and even rape. In January 2016, Human Rights Watch documented over 35 incidents of beatings by crime preventers under the guise of "citizens' arrests." The police later paraded several suspected crime preventers accused of criminal activities, prompting the issuance of an order prohibiting them from making arrests unless accompanied by uniformed officers. Nevertheless, they remained authorized to conduct surveillance, and report suspects to the police.

Much of the violence surrounding the 2016 elections was attributed to CPP operatives.[42] While the government defended the program as a community policing initiative that deterred electoral violence, critics—and even some former members—acknowledged that crime preventers were deployed primarily for political mobilization rather than public safety. Several recalled being tasked to work as party agents, grassroots mobilizers, and campaign operatives in towns and villages. The CPP's expansive reach gave the NRM an unparalleled rural presence. According to official figures, the police deployed 30 crime preventers in each of Uganda's 57,789 villages, an unprecedented penetration of state-aligned forces into everyday community life, which further blurred the line between policing and partisan politics.[43]

Numerous human rights organizations documented cases of CPP members intimidating opposition supporters, arresting them on trumped-up charges, and using violence to suppress their mobilization efforts.[44] These reports directly contradicted the government's portrayal of crime preventers as non-partisan, community-based crime watchers.[45] Opposition parties have argued instead that the program functioned as a covert instrument of repression and voter manipulation. This interpretation was inadvertently reinforced by a senior NRM official who openly boasted that "the electoral contest is over because the NRM has managed to recruit 12 million voters and disguised them as crime preventers"—a statement that underscored the program's fusion of policing, patronage, and partisan advantage.[46]

Evading Responsibility and Institutionalizing Fear

As former insurgents transitioning into state leaders, the NRA prioritized rebuilding the national army, police, prison services, and public administration. These reconstituted institutions subsequently became pillars of the NRM's consolidation of authority and prolonged incumbency. Since 2002, substantial portions of the national budget have been allocated to defense, with emphasis on expanding, training, and equipping the army, police, and intelligence services. The NRM justified these investments by citing the need to reconstruct governance infrastructure in a post-conflict context. Presently, Uganda possesses one of the most capable and expansive security apparatuses in the region, with operational reach extending from the national to the village level.

Given the sophistication and reach of Uganda's formal security apparatus, the regime's persistent reliance on third-party vigilante groups to counter opposition mobilization appears, at first glance, perplexing. The continued deployment of such irregular forces alongside the military and police raises critical questions about the strategic logic underpinning this choice. Like other authoritarian regimes, the NRM regularly uses the army and police to suppress mass protests, yet the parallel use of vigilantes suggests a deliberate effort to expand coercive capacity while blurring the boundaries between state and non-state violence. This hybrid approach not only complicates accountability and shields the regime from direct blame for abuses but also embeds coercion more deeply into everyday communal life. In doing so, it reinforces the state's ostensible monopoly on legitimate violence and contributes to the cycles of mistrust, polarization, and latent instability that have long shaped Uganda's political order.

To understand the NRM's dual reliance on vigilantes alongside its formal security apparatus, it is essential to situate this practice within the evolving challenges the regime has faced since 2001. Despite frequent deployment of the police and military—using tear gas, live ammunition, and water cannons—popular protests have persisted. Far from quelling dissent, such heavy-handed tactics have often deepened domestic discontent and invited international condemnation for human rights abuses. President Museveni has long cultivated an image as a reliable regional ally for Western powers, particularly the United States in the fight against international terrorism, a relationship that has yielded substantial military aid and training for the Ugandan army.[47] Yet his protracted rule has been marred by persistent criticism over systemic violence against civilians, including torture, enforced disappearances, and extrajudicial detentions. This tension between the need to maintain international legitimacy and the desire to preserve unchallenged domestic control helps explain the regime's turn to irregular forces whose operations can be more easily denied or disavowed.

To mitigate reputational damage while maintaining domestic control, the regime has increasingly relied on non-state actors. Vigilante groups, functioning as auxiliary enforcement units, were established with the backing of senior officials, including the Coordinator of Intelligence Services, the Inspector General of Police, and the Chief of Defence Forces. As one NRM insider explained, the goal was not to "supplant the police or army, but to cultivate a civilian force capable of suppressing dissent with lower visibility and reduced diplomatic fallout."[48] Typically armed with sticks rather than firearms, these groups are framed as civilians confronting acts of criminality, thereby making repression less visible and seemingly less lethal.

The strategic use of vigilantes enables the NRM to obscure state complicity in politically motivated violence. Official narratives depict groups such as the Kiboko Squad and Crime Preventers as grassroots security initiatives led by civilians. For instance, following violent incidents at the Clock Tower, state officials denied involvement, attributing the violence to concerned citizens.[49] The absence of uniformed personnel provided the regime with plausible deniability. Given Uganda's traumatic history with state violence, public aversion to military interventions against civilians remains strong. Concurrently, the regime faces sustained pressure from civil society, the media, and international actors whenever state forces are implicated in abuses.

Despite warnings from scholars and analysts regarding the security risks posed by vigilante groups—particularly in Uganda's ethnically and regionally segmented politics—the NRM continues to deploy them.[50] The regime perceives vigilantes as critical tools for surveilling, identifying, and neutralizing opposition actors. Their embeddedness within local communities enhances their capacity for intelligence gathering and extrajudicial enforcement. Unlike state security agencies, vigilantes often operate outside legal constraints, engaging in abductions, torture, and unlawful detention. This allows the regime to outsource repression while maintaining formal deniability. As one activist noted, vigilantes "perform the regime's dirty work," providing Museveni cover to deny involvement in criminal acts.[51] Public backlash has occasionally compelled the regime to disassociate itself from vigilante excesses. For example, after the Clock Tower incident, senior officials professed ignorance of vigilante activities, despite evidence of their coordination with state agencies. Investigations often amount to performative gestures. For example, General Kale Kayihura initially disavowed the Kiboko Squad and pledged to dismantle it, only to later admit he had personally sanctioned its formation and operations.

University students and youth are routinely recruited into vigilante ranks and mobilized as "social media warriors," tasked with defaming opposition figures.[52] These operatives disseminate disinformation through local media, online platforms, and grassroots rumor networks. Activists have reported threats to their families by vigilantes, prompting some to flee the country. Relatives of political dissidents are frequently arrested under fabricated charges, including treason and terrorism.[53] In other cases, the state initiates investigations against opposition figures while vigilantes issue anonymous threats, coercing them into silence. The regime's typical response to inquiries about such abuses ranges from outright denial to claims of ignorance. In 2016, as Crime Preventers engaged in widespread repression, the government initially denied their existence—despite evidence of their training under the community policing budget. It was only after investigative journalists and advocacy by human rights organizations revealed extensive coordination with the police that the state acknowledged their role, though it continued to distance itself from their illegal conduct.[54]

The pervasive role of vigilantes exemplifies the NRM's strategy of rule through fear.[55] The visible brutality of vigilante violence serves as a stark warning to potential dissenters, while simultaneously framing Museveni as the guarantor of national stability. As a former guerrilla commander, Museveni has consistently portrayed himself as Uganda's ultimate protector, embracing the title *Ssabalwanyi* (the chief fighter).[56] He has openly affirmed the regime's readiness to deploy force, declaring the NRM the "master of violence."[57] This rhetoric not only intimidates opposition actors but also consolidates support among older generations who still remember the chaos of past regimes. Political repression under the NRM has effectively deterred many Ugandans from civic engagement, instilling fears of arrest, torture, or imprisonment. Moreover, the regime has tightened control over political expression through restrictive media laws and stringent censorship of digital communication platforms.

Uganda's history of civil conflict and contested elections—often characterized by vote rigging, intimidation, and state-sponsored violence—has eroded public confidence in democratic processes. Many Ugandans believe that President Museveni, having seized power through rebellion, will not relinquish it via electoral means. His public statements reinforce this view, as he often dismisses the possibility of electoral defeat and casts opposition attempts to oust him through elections as naïve. These narrative fosters political apathy and discourages mobilization against the regime. For instance, various citizens' surveys have shown that many Ugandans have lost hope in the possibility of a free and fair election under President Museveni's rule, particularly in light of his personalisation of power and the politicisation of security forces. A common perception among citizens is that "Museveni, who captured power through rebellion, cannot be defeated through an election because he will never allow a free and fair vote."[58]

The growing political despondency in the country is closely tied to Museveni's dismissive rhetoric regarding the possibility of political transition through electoral means. He has become the purveyor of political hopelessness, frequently declaring that a "freedom fighter" like himself "can never be defeated by any opposition party in an electoral contest."[59] On one occasion, he even questioned how his opponents could be "so naïve" as to believe that "the NRM regime can be defeated in an election it has organised."[60] Such statements are intended to demoralise, demobilise, and dissuade Ugandans from engaging in political mobilisation against NRM rule.

Although the Museveni regime has sought to publicly disassociate itself from criminal acts of vigilantes, its only does so to evade accountability for vigilante violence. Different vigilante groups, including crime preventors, Kiboko squad and Kalangala action plan operate with support from the regime. It is clear, for example, that the KAP operated under the official command structures, setting a precedent for state-sanctioned electoral violence. The Kiboko Squad, by contrast, emerged as a shadowy force whose informal composition and legal ambiguity allowed the state to disavow responsibility while reaping the benefits of its violence. Its operations—brazenly coordinated with police yet publicly denied—highlight the regime's reliance on plausible deniability as a tactic of repression. The Crime Preventers Program marked a new phase of formalization, expanding into a massive, nationwide network with clear ties to the ruling NRM party. With an estimated 12 million members, it blurred the line between policing, party mobilization, and surveillance, embedding regime loyalists into nearly every community in Uganda.

President Museveni has faced growing scrutiny from both the Ugandan public and the international donor community over the violence perpetrated by vigilantes. In response, he has occasionally withdrawn these vigilantes from visible operations, only to retrain and redeploy them during general elections. Internationally, human rights activists have increasingly targeted the U.S. government's \$1 billion in defense aid to Uganda, arguing that continued support for the UPDF is indefensible given its documented human rights abuses. In an attempt to deflect criticism, the NRM has reduced the visible role of the military in suppressing opposition mobilization, while increasingly relying on vigilante groups to stifle political dissent. Thus, the regime views these vigilantes as essential to its grip on power.

In conclusion, the evolution of vigilante formations in Uganda under the NRM rule—from the Kalangala Action Plan to the Kiboko Squad and later the Crime Preventers Program—reflects a deliberate and increasingly institutionalized strategy by the Museveni regime to consolidate power through informal coercive mechanisms. While publicly framed as instruments for maintaining public order or community policing, these groups primarily functioned to suppress dissent and foster a climate of fear that deterred civic activism and electoral competition. The NRM's reliance on vigilante networks demonstrates how authoritarian regimes can manipulate law enforcement structures and co-opt narratives of citizen participation to build extensive, loyal, and partisan political support network. Despite official claims invoking patriotism, community safety, and ideology, these formations mainly serve to ensure regime survival and marginalize political opposition. Their persistence, impunity, and integration into state institutions reveal not only the shrinking space for political pluralism in Uganda but also the transformation of the security sector into a partisan instrument of NRM governance.

The Museveni regime's strategic use of vigilante groups exemplifies how authoritarian governments can blend formal state power with informal and non-state coercive actors to maintain control. By institutionalizing these vigilantes within the state's security apparatus while preserving a degree of deniability and low visibility, the regime effectively suppresses opposition and limits political freedoms without attracting excessive domestic backlash or international condemnation. Ultimately, the regime's reliance on such hybrid coercive mechanisms reflects broader trends in authoritarian governance, where maintaining control increasingly depends on layered, adaptable, and informal instruments of repression alongside conventional state security agencies.

Notes

1. Joanna. R. (2023) "Generating Public Engagement to Control Protests: State-Managed Vigilantism in Poland." *Javnost (Ljubljana, Slovenia)* 30.3: 322–338; Omach, P. (2010). Political violence in Uganda: the role of vigilantes and militias. *The Journal of Social, Political, and Economic Studies*, *35*(4), 426–449.
2. Jackson J, Huq AZ, Bradford B, et al. (2013) "Monopolizing force? Police legitimacy and public attitudes toward the acceptability of violence." *Psychology, Public Policy, and Law* 19(4): 479–497; Haas NE, De Keijser JW, Bruinsma GJ (2014) Public support for vigilantism, confidence in police and police responsiveness. *Policing and Society* 24(2): 224–241; Nivette. A.E (2016) "Institutional ineffectiveness, illegitimacy, and public support for vigilantism in Latin America." *Criminology* 54(1): 142–175.
3. Omach, P. (2010) "Political violence in Uganda: the role of vigilantes and militias." *The Journal of Social, Political, and Economic Studies*, *35*(4), 426–449; Tapscott, Rebecca, 'Claiming Jurisdiction: Local Vigilantes and the Struggle to Consolidate

Power', *Arbitrary States: Social Control and Modern Authoritarianism in Museveni's Uganda* (Oxford, 2021; online edn, Oxford Academic, 17 June 2021).

4. Asif, M. (2023). Police legitimacy and approval of vigilante violence: The significance of anger. *Theoretical Criminology*, *27*(2), 305–325.
5. Meagher, K. (2012). "The Strength of Weak States? Non-State Security Forces and Hybrid Governance in Africa." *Development and Change*, *43*(5), 1073–1101. https://doi.org/10.1111/j.1467-7660.2012.01794; Schuberth, M. (2018). Hybrid security governance, post-election violence and the legitimacy of community-based armed groups in urban Kenya. *Journal of Eastern African Studies*, *12*(2), 386–404. https://doi.org/10.1080/17531055.2018.1457277.
6. Schuberth, M. (2018). "Hybrid security governance, post-election violence and the legitimacy of community-based armed groups in urban Kenya." *Journal of Eastern African Studies*, *12*(2), 386–404. https://doi.org/10.1080/17531055.2018.1457277.
7. Nyiayaana, K. (2015). "Arming Community Vigilantes in the Niger Delta: Implications for Peacebuilding." *African Frontiers*, 1st ed., Routledge, pp. 131–41.
8. The East African (2015). "Between Besigye and Museveni Uganda's struggles are far from over" January 22. https://www.theeastafrican.co.ke/tea/magazine/between-besigye-and-museveni-uganda-s-struggles-are-far-from-over--1331810.
9. Price, S. (2005). "Uganda: the return of the great contender." In *New African (London. 1978)* pp. 446, pp. 22-).
10. Price, S. (2006). Uganda: "Better the devil you know..." In *New African (London. 1978)* 450: pp. 40.
11. See the documentation of Pro-government militia in Uganda database: https://militiasdb.sowi.uni-mannheim.de/militias-public/pgag/199/evidence/.
12. Rukooko, A. B., & Francis, D. J. (2005). "Protracted Civil War, Civil Militias and Political Transition in Uganda since 1986." In *Civil Militia* (1st ed., pp. 213–230). Routledge.
13. New Vision "No Reason for stopping Kalangala Action Plan" March 4, 2005. https://www.newvision.co.ug/news/1129822/reason-stopping-kalangala-action-plan.

14. African Press Organization (2022) "Hundreds 'Disappeared,' Tortured: Shut Down Illegal Detention Facilities, Ensure Justice for Victims".
15. New Vision (2002) "Mutale Defends KAPS group." April 18. https://www.newvision.co.ug/news/1058685/major-mutale-defends-kap#google_vignette.
16. Interview with ex- KAP member.
17. New Vision., ibid.
18. New Vision., ibid.
19. Interview with two MPs on defense and internal affairs committee of parliament.
20. The Observer (2017) "Kiboko squad gives police and Uganda a bad name" March 1. https://observer.ug/viewpoint/kiboko-squad-gives-police-and-uganda-a-bad-name/.
21. New Vision (2010) "Police Disown Kiboko Squad" June 10. https://www.newvision.co.ug/news/1288643/police-disown-kiboko-squad.
22. Human Rights Watch Report (2011) "Uganda: Events of 2010". https://www.hrw.org/world-report/2011/country-chapters/uganda.
23. The Monitor (2010) "Who are the faces behind the Kiboko Squad" June 26. https://www.monitor.co.ug/uganda/special-reports/who-are-the-faces-behind-kiboko-squad--1474544.
24. The Independent (2009) "Kiboko Squad Revealed" September 15. https://www.independent.co.ug/kiboko-squad-revealed/.
25. The Independent (2009) September 15. Ibid.
26. The Monitor (2007) "Museveni Praises Kiboko Squad" April 20. https://allafrica.com/stories/200704200284.html.
27. The Monitor (2013) "Kiboko Squad in Resurfaces in City Chaos" November 25. https://www.monitor.co.ug/uganda/news/national/kiboko-squad-resurfaces-in-city-chaos-1559420.
28. The Monitor. Ibid. November 25, 2013.
29. The Independent (2011) "Security forces fear more Kiboko squads" March 18. https://allafrica.com/stories/201103211430.html.
30. Uganda Radio Network (2011) "Kiboko Squad Leader Arrested" February 28. https://ugandaradionetwork.net/story/kiboko-squad-leader-arrested?districtId=729.

31. The New Vision (2011) "Police Release Kiboko Squad Leader" March 03. https://www.newvision.co.ug/news/1015435/police-release-kiboko-squad-leader.
32. Chandia Steven (2011) "Police Release Kiboko Squad Leader" New vision March 3. https://www.newvision.co.ug/news/1015435/police-release-kiboko-squad-leader.
33. Chandia Steven (11). ibid.
34. Vokes, R., & Wilkins, S. (2016). Party, patronage and coercion in the NRM'S 2016 re-election in Uganda: imposed or embedded? *Journal of Eastern African Studies*, *10*(4), 581–600.
35. Press release from Uganda Police April 4, 2014.
36. Abrahamsen, R., & Bareebe, G. (2016). Ibid.
37. Uganda Police statement, August 18, 2015.
38. Collord M. (2018) "How Uganda's government steered another state-controlled election" February 19. *The Conversation.*
39. Tapscott (2016). ibid.
40. Interview with Ahmed Katerega, the RDC for Masaka district.
41. Interview with Moses Tumuhaise, a CPP recruit from Mbarara district.
42. Oloka-Onyango, J., & Ahikire, J. (2017). *Controlling consent: Uganda's 2016 elections*. Africa World.
43. Gibb, R. (2016). The Elections in Uganda, February 2016. *Afrikaspectrum*, *51*(2), 93–101. https://doi.org/10.1177/000203971605100020.
44. Human Rights Watch (2016). ibid.
45. Al Jazeera (2026) "Is the Uganda government 'bleeding a Moster?'" February 17. https://www.aljazeera.com/features/2016/2/17/is-the-ugandan-government-breeding-a-monster.
46. Interview with a senior NRM official.
47. Interview with Nicholas Opio. Ibid.
48. Interview with a senior NRM officer, July 23, 2021.
49. ibid.
50. Omach, P. (2010). Political violence in Uganda: the role of vigilantes and militias. *The Journal of Social, Political, and Economic Studies*, *35*(4), 426–449.
51. Interview with Ingrid Turinawe, former FDC Women League Chair and Chief Mobiliser of Activists for Change (A4C).
52. Uganda Police Press Statement, August 11, 2014.

53. Kakuba, S. J. (2021). State Repression and Democratic Dispensation in Uganda 1996–2016.
54. Newsweek (2016). "Wo are Uganda's crime preventors" Jan 14. https://www.newsweek.com/who-are-ugandas-crime-preventers-415704.
55. Ssali Henry (2007). "Why there is Fear of Kiboko Brigade" *The Monitor*, April 22. https://allafrica.com/stories/200704220119.html.
56. The Monitor (2017). "I am not Anyone's Servant." January 27. https://www.monitor.co.ug/uganda/news/national/i-am-not-anyone-s-servant-says-museveni-1685490.
57. Sadam K. Kitatatta (2017). "NRM is the Master of Violence––Museveni" The Observer, October 18. https://observer.ug/news/headlines/55479-nrm-is-the-master-of-violence-museveni.
58. Interview with Moses Byamugisha, former FDC party presidential contestant.
59. The Monitor, February 2, 2021. https://www.monitor.co.ug/uganda/special-reports/elections/nrm-can-t-lose-museveni-1640460.
60. The Monitor (2021). "No group can deafeat NRM-Museveni" February 8. https://www.monitor.co.ug/uganda/news/national/no-group-can-defeat-nrm-museveni-3283418.

CHAPTER 8

Rethinking Postwar Authoritarianism: Lessons and Implications from the NRM Regime

Reflections on the Resilience of the NRM's Civil-Authoritarian Regime

Authoritarian regimes have been shown to rely on a range of strategies for resilience and survival. These strategies are broadly categorized into coercive and non-coercive. Coercive strategies involve the use of the security apparatus to maintain control and suppress or eliminate dissent. They include acts such as surveillance, intimidation, arbitrary arrests, torture, and military deployments. Regimes may also deploy legal mechanisms—such as anti-terrorism laws, restrictions on freedom of speech and assembly, and broad sedition laws—to criminalize political opposition, curtail media freedom, and restrict the activities of civil society organizations. Such legal repression allows authoritarian rulers to sustain their durability in power.

Noncoercive strategies involve softer mechanisms of control, such as co-optation, political accommodation, patronage networks, clientelism, and even selective concessions to rivals. The NRM regime, under Museveni has mastered the art of this approach by often incorporating opposition parties, civic associations, and traditional and religious institutions into its broader political coalition. This strategy serves to neutralize alternative centers of power while projecting an image of inclusivity and pluralism. Through material inducements, appointments to government

G. Bareebe, *Social Structures and the Making of Museveni's Civil-Authoritarian Regime in Uganda*,
https://doi.org/10.1007/978-3-032-14015-9_8

positions, and the selective distribution of state resources, the regime effectively co-opts potential critics, transforming them into stakeholders in the system. By blurring the boundaries between state and party, the NRM ensures that loyalty is rewarded, dissent is discouraged, and the political space remains tightly controlled without always resorting to excessive totalitarianism.

Therefore, the resilience of the NRM's authoritarian regime under President Museveni is a function of a unique interplay between coercive force, residual social structures, and militarized patronage networks which have all shaped regime consolidation since 1986. Contrary to dominant narratives that emphasize the dominance of repression in authoritarian durability, the Ugandan case reveals a more complex reality. Museveni's regime has consistently relied on a hybrid governance strategy that combines military coercion with societal incorporation, co-optation, and selective compromise. Entrenched social actors—such as traditional kingdoms, churches, and landed elites—have not only survived postwar authoritarian rule but have actively shaped key policy outcomes, often compelling the regime to govern through negotiation and accommodation arrangements. This hybrid model has allowed the NRM to neutralize potential challengers while maintaining a façade of inclusion and legitimacy.

In many ways, the NRM regime was compelled to adopt a blend of coercive and non-coercive strategies by the presence of entrenched social groups whose willingness to defend their interests significantly shaped the regime's approach to governance. Unlike postwar regimes such as Paul Kagame's RPF in Rwanda, which inherited a political landscape where many social structures had been dismantled by war and genocide, the NRM inherited a country marked by the persistence of durable and politically active societal institutions. The RPF, for example, was allowed space to reconstruct the state with minimal resistance from organized social groups. In contrast, the NRM confronted pre-existing networks of authority that could not be easily dissolved without risking political instability. Aware of such risks, the regime pursued a hybrid strategy of negotiation, co-optation, and selective repression. In doing so, it constructed an authoritarian system that relies not solely on coercion but also on societal incorporation—managing dissent by drawing influential social actors into the regime's orbit while neutralizing their autonomy and influence.

Since 1986, regime stability in Uganda has been fundamentally reinforced by the NRM's ability to manage and incorporate influential social actors, transforming potential challengers into political partners. A notable example is the regime's retreat from the proposed Regional Tier system in the face of strong opposition from monarchies and landed elites. The outcome underscores how entrenched social groups have not only survived under NRM's authoritarian rule but have actively shaped critical policy outcomes. Similarly, on the contentious issue of land tenure, the NRM relied on dialogue, negotiation, and strategic concessions rather than outright coercion. These responses reflect a pragmatic recognition that long-term authoritarian stability requires flexibility in governance and sensitivity to the enduring power of societal groups.

Although the NRM frequently deploys repression against its opponents—particularly the political opposition and defiant social actors, as exemplified by the Buganda riots and the Rwenzururu crisis, it has consistently resorted to negotiations and compromise to manage its relationships with entrenched social groups. In both the Buganda and Rwenzururu cases, military interventions were swiftly followed by dialogue, reflecting the regime's recognition that coercion alone cannot resolve deep-rooted societal tensions. While the state retains a strong coercive apparatus, NRM leaders have come to understand that durable governance requires more than repression. The persistence and autonomy of powerful social groups have constrained the regime's reliance on coercive rule and compelled it to adopt a complex hybrid strategy that blends repression with accommodation. Uganda's experience thus demonstrates that even within authoritarian systems, the structure and resilience of social groups can profoundly shape regime behavior and governance strategies.

The outcome of NRM's governance approach is best understood as a civil-authoritarian regime, an authoritarian system tempered by the enduring influence of powerful, organized social groups. This hybrid arrangement was not simply a strategic choice but a structural necessity, shaped by the constraining power of Uganda's residual social structure––i.e., monarchies, landed elites, religious institutions, and other legacy actors with deep historical roots and well-defined interests. The creation of a broad-based government by the NRM was less an act of inclusivity and more a calculated move to pre-empt resistance by incorporating these actors into the architecture of power. While military repression remains a central tool of control—used decisively against political opposition and non-compliant social actors—the Museveni regime often finds itself navigating the gravitational pull of entrenched social power. In this way, Uganda's civil authoritarianism reflects a paradox; i.e., even in a heavily militarized regime, pre-existing social structures continues to shape policy outcomes and impose limits on the exercise of coercion.

The NRM can be contrasted with other post-conflict authoritarian regimes in the region, such as Rwanda's RPF, which underwent a similar process of regime formation and consolidation after genocide but under markedly different structural conditions. In post-genocide Rwanda, the RPF faced far fewer constraints from organized social groups. Many traditional institutions—such as churches and other social organizations—had lost credibility due to their complicity in the genocide and were politically weakened. Unlike in Uganda, where entrenched social actors retained influence and forced the regime into negotiation and power-sharing, the RPF encountered a relative power vacuum. This allowed armed elites within the RPF to construct a far more centralized and coercive state apparatus, in which military authority was the main source of regime durability and consolidation. The absence of credible social challengers enabled the RPF to fuse the state with the military and project an image—both domestically and internationally—of disciplined, centralized control as the foundation of post-genocide stability.

In light of the widespread failure of post-conflict state reconstruction and regime consolidation in many African countries, the NRM's trajectory under Museveni underscores the need for more nuanced analytical attention to the dilemmas confronting postwar state-builders. Existing scholarship on post-conflict governance often emphasizes institutional design, transitional justice, and democratization, yet insufficient attention has been paid to the underlying contradictions and trade-offs involved in constructing regimes that are simultaneously effective, durable, and perceived as legitimate. The Ugandan case illustrates that postwar regimes must navigate a complex terrain shaped by residual social structures, contested authority, and competing imperatives of coercion and co-optation. In such contexts, state-builders are compelled to forge hybrid governance strategies that blend militarized control with negotiated accommodation of influential societal actors. However, these strategies often generate internal contradictions—between centralization and decentralization, repression and responsiveness, or elite consolidation and societal incorporation—that shape both the nature of regime stability and the limits of state legitimacy. Uganda's experience thus reveals the analytical inadequacy of frameworks that treat post-conflict authoritarian consolidation as a linear or purely coercive process, calling instead for a more grounded and dynamic understanding of how regimes are embedded in, and constrained by, the social terrain of postwar societies.

This book makes key contributions to three areas in the literature on postwar governance and state reconstruction. First, the field of peacebuilding has traditionally focused on conflict resolution, institutional design, and transitional justice, while paying less attention to the question of what sustains peace and regime stability in post-conflict contexts. The durability of postwar regimes, particularly those that do not democratize, remains inadequately theorized. Second, existing scholarship has largely overlooked the strategic role of the military in post-conflict state reconstruction—not merely as a guarantor of security, but as a central instrument through which ruling elites consolidate power, rebuild state institutions, and redefine state-societal relations after war. Third, the independent role of domestic residual social structures—such as traditional authorities, religious institutions, and landed elites—in shaping the configuration and trajectory of postwar political orders is largely overlooked. Yet, as the case of Museveni's regime illustrates, the rebuilding of political, social, and economic systems in the aftermath of civil war is deeply conditioned by the presence or absence of these enduring societal formations. Far from being passive remnants of a prewar past, these actors often reassert themselves as key political interlocutors, compelling ruling regimes to govern through a mix of coercion, accommodation, and co-optation.

The focus on the residual social structure offers a novel analytical lens through which to understand post-conflict political order by highlighting the enduring influence of domestic social formations that predate the conflict and survive its aftermath. The analysis demonstrates that traditional kingdoms, religious institutions, landed elites, and other historically rooted actors are not merely passive legacies but active agents in shaping postwar governance arrangements. These groups constrain authoritarian consolidation, negotiate political inclusion, and often condition the parameters of state authority. This emphasis on the residual social structure addresses a significant gap in both peacebuilding and authoritarianism scholarship by showing how societal embeddedness—not just coercive capacity or elite strategy—can determine the form, flexibility, and durability of post-conflict regimes. In doing so, this work contributes a grounded, context-sensitive framework for analyzing regime consolidation that is focused to the social terrain upon which postwar states are built.

Yet still, despite the enduring influence of social formations, the centrality of the military in sustaining the long durability of Museveni's civil-authoritarian regime remains paramount. Following his rise to power, Museveni pledged to deepen political participation as a foundation for postwar democratization. However, over time, he has increasingly relied on the military not only to suppress dissent but also to enforce political consent—particularly in instances where co-optation, negotiation, or institutional compromise have proven insufficient. The growing entanglement of the military in partisan politics rise serious concerns about Uganda's political future, particularly in light of Museveni's advanced age and the absence of a clear succession plan. Observers have expressed concern over the role of the Special Forces Command (SFC), which operates as a highly personalized security apparatus loyal to Museveni and his son General Kainerugaba. Fears persist that the SFC could intervene militarily to install Museveni's son despite his unpopularity both within the armed forces and among the general public. Such a scenario would carry significant risks, potentially triggering elite fragmentation, civil unrest, or even widespread violence.

The Museveni regime has sought to manage anxieties over succession by asserting that any transition will be guided by the constitution. This reassurance followed growing public opposition from former senior military officers who have spoken out against dynastic succession, reminding Museveni that Uganda is not a monarchy.[1] These tensions underscore the unresolved contradictions at the heart of Uganda's political order, i.e., an authoritarian regime built on a hybrid foundation of military power and societal incorporation, now facing an unpredictable future shaped by competing forces within the military, political elite, and the public domain. As such, the post-Museveni trajectory remains highly uncertain, with multiple, and potentially destabilizing scenarios still in play.

Despite concerns raised by some former military officers, a substantial number of serving officers—particularly those in senior command positions—remain deeply loyal to the Museveni regime. This loyalty is not merely ideological but rooted in material and institutional interests. Many of these officers have a vested interest in the prolonged tenure of the regime, as their continued access to wealth, privilege and protection is tied to its survival. In return for their loyalty, the regime frequently deploys them in operations that generate opportunities for rent extraction, corruption, and resource plunder—often with impunity. These forms of economic reward are embedded within a broader patronage system that links senior military figures with political elites and business actors in a tightly knit network of mutual benefit, presided over by Museveni himself. In this arrangement, the military does not function as an autonomous institution, but as part of a larger system of political and economic exchange.

This network has been instrumental in facilitating access to illicit trade in lucrative resources such as gold, diamonds, timber, and coffee—both within Uganda and across borders. While some scholars have argued that the proliferation of such predatory networks can ultimately erode state authority or generate internal instability, Uganda's experience complicates this view. Despite widespread corruption and systemic economic plunder, the regime has remained remarkably resilient. This suggests that, under certain conditions, militarized patronage networks can serve not as sources of destabilization, but as mechanisms of regime consolidation—binding powerful actors to the state through mutually reinforcing interests. However, the long-term consequences of such arrangements for institutional development, accountability, and post-Museveni stability are largely uncertain.

Lessons and Implications Across Africa

Across the continent, the focus on post-war authoritarianism, regime consolidation and domestic social formations—particularly the residual social structure—has broader implications for understanding the relationship between the military and politics in societies recovering from prolonged civil wars and episodes of political violence. Where these residual structures are too weak or fragmented to contain the ambitions of armed elites, the likelihood of repression, military dominance, or outright coups is significantly higher. In such contexts, the military often emerges as a central political actor during transitional periods—either by installing a civilian president who serves its interests or by directly undermining elected leaders when armed elites' privileges are perceived to be at risk. Egypt's post-2011 trajectory offers a salient case. Following the revolution that ousted Hosni Mubarak, Mohamed Morsi became the country's first democratically elected president. Yet, within a year, he was overthrown in a military coup, and his party, the Muslim Brotherhood, was violently suppressed. This transition ultimately entrenched military rule under President Abdel Fattah el-Sisi. Similarly, in Zimbabwe, the military staged a "soft coup" in 2017 that removed Robert Mugabe from power. Rather than ushering in democratic reform, the coup facilitated the elevation of Mugabe's former Vice-President, Emmerson Mnangagwa, while General Constantino Chiwenga—the architect of the coup—was appointed Vice-President. The military's intervention was widely seen as a calculated effort to preserve the economic and political interests of the armed forces and allied elites. In many respects, Zimbabwe's experience parallels that of Uganda, where both Mugabe and Museveni presided over regimes that tolerated limited internal dissent and controlled political contestation. Yet this tolerance was carefully managed to prevent any serious challenge to regime hegemony—and when those limits were tested, repression was swift and uncompromising.

The nature of the post-conflict NRM regime in Uganda contrasts sharply with other regimes that underwent similar processes of postwar reconstruction, such as Rwanda's RPF and Angola's MPLA. In post-genocide Rwanda, the destruction and discrediting of churches, local elites, and civil society created a social vacuum that allowed the RPF to rapidly centralize power. With few credible societal challengers, the RPF fused the ruling party with the military and governed with minimal resistance from opposition parties or independent social actors. Similarly, Angola and Mozambique emerged from prolonged civil wars with fragmented or severely weakened traditional structures. This absence of robust societal constraints enabled ruling parties to entrench highly militarized and extractive state apparatuses. In both contexts, regimes emphasized coercive control with only narrow, instrumental accommodation of residual social institutions, producing rigid but durable forms of authoritarianism anchored in military loyalty, elite consolidation, and control over natural resources. Somewhere in between lies Zimbabwe and Ethiopia. In Zimbabwe, the ZANU-PF regime partially incorporated traditional leaders while undermining their autonomy, using patronage and land redistribution as tools of authoritarian consolidation. Ethiopia's TPLF-led regime institutionalized residual ethno-regional identities through federalism, granting local elites partial autonomy while using coercion to suppress dissent. However, this strategy eventually collapsed under the weight of rising ethnic nationalism. In contrast, Uganda's NRM has maintained a more stable, though equally authoritarian, regime by continually negotiating with entrenched societal actors and adapting its coercive strategies to the constraints imposed by these social groups, further highlighting how the strength and persistence of residual social structures shape not only the type of authoritarianism that emerges but also its long-term stability and adaptability.

Note

1. Otafiire, ibid.

FSC
www.fsc.org
MIX
Papier | Fördert
gute Waldnutzung
FSC® C083411

Kolibri 360 GmbH
Ferdinand-Jühlke-Straße 7
99095 Erfurt, Deutschland
produktsicherheit@kolibri360.de